WITHDRAWN

An Evaluation of the
Soviet Profit Reforms

PRAEGER SPECIAL STUDIES IN
INTERNATIONAL ECONOMICS AND DEVELOPMENT

An Evaluation of the Soviet Profit Reforms

WITH SPECIAL REFERENCE TO AGRICULTURE

David W. Conklin

PRAEGER PUBLISHERS
New York • Washington • London

The purpose of Praeger Special Studies is to make specialized research in U.S. and international economics and politics available to the academic, business, and government communities. For further information, write to the Special Projects Division, Praeger Publishers, Inc., 111 Fourth Avenue, New York, N.Y. 10003.

PRAEGER PUBLISHERS
111 Fourth Avenue, New York, N.Y. 10003, U.S.A.
5, Cromwell Place, London S.W.7, England

Published in the United States of America in 1970
by Praeger Publishers, Inc.

Library of Congress Catalog Card Number: 74-122082

Printed in the United States of America

To Marilyn

ACKNOWLEDGMENTS

This book has developed from my Ph.D. thesis, written at the Massachusetts Institute of Technology. In view of this, I wish to express my sincere appreciation to the professors on my thesis committee--Evsey D. Domar, Edwin Kuh, and the late Max Millikan. Their friendly encouragement, general guidance, and specific criticisms proved extremely valuable. I also wish to thank Alvin Harman, now at RAND, and Eytan Sheshinski, a professor at Hebrew University, for their comments on early drafts of the thesis. The Canada Council, the Ford Foundation, the Massachusetts Institute of Technology, and the University of Western Ontario provided much appreciated financial support.

My colleagues at the University of Western Ontario have made many helpful suggestions concerning the various arguments and analyses presented in this book. I am indebted to them for their assistance in this regard. I would like to thank Mrs. M. Gower for typing the manuscript. To my wife, Marilyn, and my family I wish to express gratitude for support throughout the writing of this book.

CONTENTS

Chapter

Chapter

LIST OF TABLES AND FIGURES

TABLES

FIGURES

GLOSSARY

kolkhoz	Collective or cooperative farm.
khozraschet	Economic accountability.
kopeck	1/100 of one ruble.
oblast	A territorial administrative division within a republic of the Soviet Union.
ruble (R)	The equivalent of 100 kopecks.
sovkhoz	State- or government-owned farm.
sovnarkhoz	Regional planning organization.

An Evaluation of the Soviet Profit Reforms

CHAPTER **1** THE ANALYTICAL
FRAMEWORK AND BASIC
ARGUMENT

SHORTCOMINGS AND
INTERENTERPRISE PLANNING

Russia's leaders have decided that the kind of central
planning instituted by Stalin in 1928 is not appropriate for
their economy today. The first part of this book discusses
the shortcomings of the economic system instituted by Stalin
and maintained until 1965. This discussion focuses on the
agricultural production process, as Russian agriculture provides a unified set of examples in which the nature of these
shortcomings can easily be understood. The second part of
this book analyzes the shift from detailed central planning to
a new system that seeks to combine central planning with decentralized decision making. The government participates in
setting of prices and the formulation of general guidelines,
while profit maximization is to be an important goal of local
decision making. Analysis of the new planning framework requires the development of new economic theory. In the exploration of this theory, the author concludes that many significant
questions cannot be answered on a theoretical basis alone.
Actual experience is necessary to determine the influence of
alternative government policies. This emphasizes the importance of the Russian "experiments"--not only for Russia,
but also for the West.
    Western nations have experienced an increasing economic
intervention by the government, and yet they have maintained
the desire for decentralized initiative and responsibility.
National policies in regard to depressed regions, urban renewal, housing, new cities, pollution, scientific research,
agricultural incomes, transportation systems, and mineral
exploration often provide financial incentives; but the national
government is not involved in the detailed planning or execu-
tion of each project or program. In my opinion, alternative
methods of combining central guidelines with local decision

1

making are becoming increasingly important in both Russia
and the West. From this viewpoint, the examination of the
Russian economy acquires a new and enriched meaning.

By 1965, the Soviet leadership had decided that their nation should embark on a new economic course. Their statements indicated a thorough dissatisfaction with previous
central-planning practices and declared a need to expand the
initiative, rights, and responsibilities of individual economic
enterprises. A. N. Kosygin, chairman of the Union of Soviet
Socialist Republics (U.S.S.R.) Council of Ministers, made
the following comments, for example:

> The economic initiative and rights of enterprises
> are constricted and they have insufficient responsi-
> bility. . . .
>
>   It is necessary to create conditions in which
> enterprises can decide questions of improving their
> production independently and will be interested in
> making better use of the production capital allocated
> to them for increasing output and profits. This ne-
> cessitates leaving to the enterprises more funds
> from their profits so that they can develop produc-
> tion, perfect technology, offer material incentives
> to personnel and improve the working conditions
> and everyday life of their workers and employees.
> . . . Along with this, nonreturnable state-financed
> capital investments should be limited and the use of
> credit expanded. [1]

The kind of central planning instituted by Stalin has continually encountered three problems: an information problem,
a coordination problem, and a flexibility problem. A major
argument of this book is that these problems have increased
in both difficulty and importance as Russia's economy has
become more developed. Changes in technology that can
affect both the quality and the cost of a product have become
permanent features of all modern economies and appear
essential for their progress. Such technological changes have
compounded the information, coordination, and flexibility
problems of the Stalinist central-planning system to such an
extent that this system is being rejected. Other kinds of
central planning may be better able to make those decisions
that concern the quality and the cost of products.

The Stalinist system has experienced difficulty in trans-
ferring appropriate and accurate information from each
enterprise to the central planners. On the technical side, a
difficulty arises because some aspects of production cannot
be quantified easily or precisely. This is true of many aspects

of product quality. It is most obvious in cases where the
relative desirability of different product characteristics depends upon the preferences of consumers. Even with products
purchased by industries, the central planners have experienced considerable difficulty in obtaining information concerning quality, digesting this information, deciding upon
future changes in quality, and imposing their decisions concerning these changes. This predicament is perplexing when
considering a known spectrum of product characteristics.
Its perplexity is compounded when planners consider the
possibility of innovation to create a new and improved product,
designed to serve some specific purpose better than the
existing product could, or when they consider an innovation
designed to reduce production costs. The precise results of
a future innovation cannot easily be predicted. This uncertainty means that information sent to central planners may
not be appropriate or accurate, and so the planners' decisions,
based on this information, may be improper.

There is a human side to this information problem as
well as a technical side. An enterprise may consciously send
inaccurate information to the central planners, so that the
planners will make decisions favoring this particular enterprise. The enterprise may underestimate its production
potential, so that it will be given low production quotas that
it can easily fulfill. The enterprise may claim it is manufacturing high-quality merchandise while it is actually reducing its cost by lowering quality. In this way, actions that
are contrary to the public good may be rewarded, and the
quantity and quality of the nation's output may be unnecessarily
low.

Under the system of central planning instituted by Stalin,
production plans have not been coordinated satisfactorily.
Confusion and delays resulting from this coordination problem
have reduced production below its potential levels. Central
planners have not been able to cope flawlessly with the technical difficulty of reconciling and adjusting the production
plans of every enterprise. Present methods of data analysis
in Russia have not been capable of achieving the goal of
synchronizing all demands for each product with all supplies
of each product. Hence, even if the information problem
were solved, this inability to coordinate all production plans
would lead to demands for reform of the economic system.
In a sense, each quality variation creates a new product.
For purposes of allocation, each variety of a product must
be placed in a separate category if it is to go to the customers
for whom it is most appropriate. Each variety of a product

may also require a different set of inputs. Thus technological change that expands the quality spectrum, or creates new products, tends to complicate the coordination problem.

A third problem arises from the fact that, for many enterprises, no one can predict the output and necessary inputs precisely. Enterprise workers may increase their efforts. Unforeseen technological change may occur. Droughts or floods may disrupt plans. Machinery may have to be repaired or replaced unexpectedly. Centrally determined plans must be changed to take such variations into account if delays, confusion, and excess inventories are to be avoided. Russia's central planners have experienced considerable difficulty in this sphere; their methods and decisions have lacked the flexibility that the solution of this problem requires. To progress at its fastest possible rate, the economic system must not only be able to adjust to technological change, it must foster technological change. When an enterprise is faced with rigid plans in regard to the inputs it receives and the output it must produce, then the opportunity for local initiative in either quality modification or cost-reducing innovation is severely restricted. In this regard, the Stalinist type of central planning conflicts with the need, increasingly emphasized by Russia's leaders, for involvement of all personnel in the efforts to improve production techniques. Hence the growing importance of technological change acts to intensify the problem of flexibility as well as the problems of information and coordination.

In the following chapters, the quality of a product is interpreted broadly to include any variation in the nature of a product. The quality of a product is not a one-dimensional aspect. Modern products possess many different characteristics, any one of which may be altered by the producer. A modern machine may consist of hundreds of parts, each of which is subject to modification. In an ideal economic system, different enterprises may produce different quality products even if they possess the same production information. In fact, any one firm may produce goods that differ markedly in quality. Such situations may arise because different customers may prefer or even require different quality products. The "best quality" product from the view of one customer may not be the "best quality" product for the needs of another customer. This is clearly the case with goods consumed directly by the people where subjective evaluations and differences in fashion styles may vary greatly within the population and over time.

There is considerable evidence that Soviet leaders have become increasingly concerned with the satisfaction of consumers and sincerely desire to cater to consumer preferences more than they have in the past. This means that the quality of goods is acquiring new significance. But, for central planners, information concerning quality is difficult to obtain. This is true of both production and consumption information. The myriad of possible modifications an enterprise may make in its products complicates tremendously the cost data sent to central planners. A complete evaluation of consumer preferences would require that detailed information be obtained from every citizen or at least from a considerable sample. Hence the increasing concern for the Russian consumer has presented a task that the Stalinist kind of central planning has not been able to solve.

We might speculate that the inability to cope with this new task in the consumer sphere will become more noticeable as per capita incomes grow. At early stages of development, consumer purchases are concentrated on primary products. With higher incomes, consumers spend an increasing proportion of their money on industrial goods or services. It may be suggested that the latter are susceptible to more quality modification than are primary products. In addition, consumers may desire to spend their higher incomes on better quality products rather than simply more of the same products. Hence the significance of quality may be expected to increase and, with this, the shortcomings of central planners may become more evident.

The first part of this book is concerned with intermediate or enterprise customers rather than with final consumption. At this level the problems surrounding quality are not as obvious as they are with regard to consumer preferences. It is a purpose of this book to emphasize that serious quality problems do exist at the interenterprise level, quite apart from the problems caused by the subjective nature of consumer preferences. The quality of inputs and of outputs is an extremely important element in the production processes of modern enterprises. The Stalinist type of central planning, with its information, coordination, and flexibility problems, has not been able to deal satisfactorily with quality even at the interenterprise level.

THE AGRICULTURAL
PRODUCTION PROCESS

A description of the Soviet agricultural production process
in the 1950's and 1960's serves to illustrate the nature and
extent of the above-mentioned shortcomings in interenterprise
planning. The exposition in the following chapters is based
on a broad view of the production process--a view that in-
cludes industries supplying agriculture with necessary equipment and materials, farming itself, and the marketing of
agricultural products. An advantage of concentrating on agriculture is that technical details concerning interenterprise
relationships can be grasped without prior knowledge of
science or engineering. The interenterprise relationships
are relatively clear-cut and few in number. Aspects of quality
are not complex. Hence the discussions in the Soviet press--
to which this commentary frequently refers--are meaningful
even for the uninitiated.
    It has not been my intention to present a complete account
of the characteristics of Soviet agriculture or of the events
that have affected it. Rather, my purpose has been to provide
a coherent set of examples of the shortcomings that have
arisen with detailed central planning and that underlie the recent profit reforms. This has been necessary as a background
for the analysis of the reforms in the second part of the book.
Nevertheless, the description of the Soviet agricultural production process is important in itself. It appears that Russia's
leaders have been far more disappointed with their nation's
agricultural performance than with its industrial accomplish-
ments. Plans and hopes for the agricultural sector have been
frustrated repeatedly. The following chapters concentrate on
three aspects of agriculture: attempts to increase the output
and improve the effectiveness of chemical fertilizers; efforts
to expand the area of irrigated land and enrich its usefulness;
and repeated endeavors to modify farm machinery so that it
will be more appropriate for the various tasks it must perform
as well as for the different climates and soil conditions within
which it must operate. These aspects have not been investigated to any great extent in the writings of Western economic
commentators, yet they are considered extremely important
by the Soviet leadership. In 1964, for example, the Plenary
Session of the Communist Party of the Soviet Union (CPSU)
Central Committee declared:

Implementation of the planned measures for intensification of agricultural production should proceed in
three chief directions: First, along the broad chemicalization of farming and animal husbandry. . . .
Second, along the path of the comprehensive development of irrigated farming . . . Third, along the
path of introducing integrated mechanization. . . .
The intensive conduct of agriculture presupposes
the widest introduction of the achievements of science
and advanced experience in production. The chief
goal is to make the best achievements of domestic
and foreign science and advanced labor methods the
property of the millions of toilers of the countryside. [2]

Such quotations illustrate the Soviet leadership's concern
over how each ton of chemical fertilizer, each ruble invested
in irrigation or drainage, and each piece of farm machinery
can be made more effective. This concern with quality and
technological change, experienced throughout the Soviet
economy, has motivated the profit reforms. As we look at
each of chemical fertilizer, irrigation and drainage, and
farm machinery, we shall see that persistent barriers to
technological improvements have been embedded in the Stalinist
type of central planning. To achieve the desired technological
advances, the problems of information, coordination, and
flexibility must be overcome--either through some revolution
in computer machinery and techniques, or through the decentralization of decision making. At present, the latter
offers the greatest hope, and so it is upon the profit reforms
that today's leaders are relying.

In the Soviet press, nearly every article concerning
chemical fertilizer mentions three shortcomings. (1) Fertilizers are not processed in such a way as to prevent deterioration in the time interval between production and use. (2) They
are not concentrated so as to reduce costs of transportation
and application; that is, useless ballast makes up more of their
weight and volume than is necessary. (3) Production of compound fertilizers--containing nitrogen, phosphorous, and
potassium instead of only one of these nutrients--is too small
a proportion of total production.

When we investigate the reasons for these shortcomings
we shall encounter the difficulties experienced by detailed
central planning in the sphere of interenterprise relationships.
The agricultural production process extends from the farm
back to the distributors and producers of chemical fertilizers.
The ability of these distributors and producers to provide

farms with the most appropriate types of fertilizers depends
to a major extent upon the machinery and equipment that they
receive from the machine-building firms. These firms depend upon the design institutes for the detailed blueprints
upon which they may base their modifications in fertilizer-
producing machinery. The design institutes, in turn, often
rely upon the scientific-research institutes for knowledge
concerning the various chemical processes that might be
adopted.

In the past, the scientific-research institutes have not
been familiar with the actual requirements of Russia's farms
and chemical-producing enterprises. Their activities have
been geared to a basic research that has failed to provide design institutes with clear recommendations concerning current
problems. The design institutes, on the other hand, have not
been able to conduct the scientific research necessary for significant improvements in the production of chemical products.
In addition, the design institutes have not been aware of the
precise needs of each machine-building firm. Repeatedly,
the Soviet press has cited examples of firms receiving blueprints that have been inappropriate and that have resulted in
costly errors or delays.

The successful operation of the machine-building enterprises has been restricted by this lack of assistance from
research and design institutes. Hence the failure of chemical-
producing firms to receive equipment necessary for improvements in their products can, to a significant degree, be traced
back to shortcomings in the performance of research and design institutes. The machine-building enterprises, themselves, have added to this problem of inappropriate equipment.
In the past, they have received no premium for producing
equipment of high quality. On the contrary, the success indicators, on which their performance has been evaluated,
have discouraged attempts to improve quality. Maximization
of output specified in quantity terms and minimization of cost
can lead, in fact, to a conscious production of equipment that
prevents improvement in the final chemical product. The
machine-building firm may seem to be doing a fine job on the
basis of established evaluation criteria, yet it may be seriously
hampering the chemical producers. In the past, these producers have not been free to choose among alternative equipment suppliers, nor has the price system allowed price
gradations based on the many qualitative aspects of machinery.
Hence the customer has not been able to restrict its purchases
to producers with a reputation for high quality, nor has the

customer been able legally to offer a higher price for better than customary quality.

This lack of concern for the customer's needs is found, in turn, in the attitude of the chemical producers towards the Soviet farms that purchase their fertilizers. Again the criteria upon which enterprise success has been evaluated have discouraged attempts to make the product more advantageous or useful for the customer. State standards have existed in regard to quality, but these have clearly failed. The central planners have not been able to obtain information with enough detail and precision to include this information in an evaluation of each firm's economic performance. In reply to charges of negligence, a firm can pass the blame backwards to those enterprises that failed to supply it with the equipment or other inputs necessary to improve the product's quality. The difficulty of coordination hampers any clear decision as to how the responsibility for inadequate quality should be shared. Technological progress entails an ever-changing set of product standards, and so the flexibility problem complicates this aspect of central planning even further.

Problems connected with the supply of chemical fertilizers have received prominent notice in the Soviet press throughout the 1950's and 1960's. A more recent program is that of extending irrigation and drainage systems. Emphasis on irrigation and drainage has become obvious only since 1965. Brezhnev has noted that in the twenty years from 1946 to 1965 the state invested only 5.6 billion rubles in the construction of water-resource systems for agriculture, yet the 1966 to 1970 Five Year Plan has provided for an investment of over 10 billion rubles in this sector.[3] The goal of expanding the area of farmland improved by irrigation or drainage has been presented in the atmosphere of a national campaign. A rapid and thorough mobilization has been requested by Russia's political leaders--a mobilization to double the total acreage that has been improved in this manner in the ten years between 1965 and 1975.

This projected advance has been hampered by the same types of difficulties that have been mentioned in regard to increasing the effectiveness of chemical fertilizers. For the irrigation and drainage sector to progress, it is necessary that all interrelated industries progress as well. Officials responsible for this program have criticized severely the poor quality of equipment with which they must construct and operate their water systems. They cite the need for more appropriate types of machinery and for improvements in the technical designs of such systems. Here again, the problems

of information, coordination, and flexibility impede the
attainment of the desired transformation. The construction
organizations themselves have been blamed for a lack of concern for the quality of their irrigation and drainage systems.
Such organizations have not been responsible to their customers, the farms; and the officials to whom they have been
responsible have not been able to exert the detailed control
necessary to develop such a concern for the farms' needs.

When we turn from irrigation and drainage to the wide
range of farm machinery and equipment, we find the continual
reappearance of this gap between the organizations responsible
for an innovation and the farms which must use the results of
that innovation. This is the case, for example, in regard to
creation of new machinery and equipment appropriate for the
arid climate of the Virgin Lands, a new agricultural area into
which Khrushchev directed an eastward migration in the 1950's.
The provision of new safety mechanisms for farm machinery,
the development of more powerful tractors, and the expansion
of rural electrification facilities provide additional instances
where the gap between enterprises has hampered improvement in quality. Previous changes in the planning structure
have failed to bridge this gap effectively. The All-Union
Farm Machinery Association was created in 1961, for example,
to supervise the development of new agricultural equipment
and techniques. In this role, it has operated a network of
machine-testing stations. Yet the gap has continued to bother
Soviet experts in agricultural matters.

In the argument of this book, quality is considered in a
broad sense, as including all the relevant aspects of a commodity. As we have noted, the appropriateness of a commodity
for a particular task and modifications to cope successfully
with new tasks have repeatedly created difficulties for centralized decision making. The provision of spare parts for a
commodity is another aspect that has troubled central planners.
Throughout the Soviet economy, criticism has been raised
concerning shortages of spare parts. Manufacturing firms
may find it easier to fulfill their gross-output plan by constructing complete units the gross value of which contains a
larger component of supplies purchased outside the plant and
a smaller component of value added than do spare parts.
That is, the gross value added per unit of value may be higher
for complete units than for spare parts. To take care of
numerous small orders for specific types of spare parts may
simply require more man-hours per unit of value added and,
therefore, higher costs than are required per unit of value

added for complete units. Agricultural officials have criticized the shortage of spare parts often and bitterly. Many
firms that fulfill the output plan for spare parts in terms of
total ruble value have seemed unconcerned about the assortment
plan, so that while some parts are available, other equally
vital parts are not.

   Criticisms concerning farm machinery and equipment
used in the fields reappear in discussions concerning machinery and equipment for marketing and processing agricultural
products. The raising of cattle has been expanded, for
example, but special facilities for transporting cattle have
not been built. The problems of information, coordination,
and flexibility have been particularly acute in regard to
perishable foods. For many farm products, shortcomings
in the system of transportation can result in major or even
total destruction of the value of the product. The gap between
farms on the one hand and the transportation and state marketing authorities on the other has been especially serious in this
regard. It is a commonplace that the kolkhoz or collective
farm markets, where state transportation and marketing
authorities do not intervene between producer and consumer,
sell much higher quality products than do the state organizations. Yet it is not clear that the traditional collective-
farm markets, if expanded, could provide efficiently for the
agricultural needs of all the Soviet urban population. A
reasonable approach is to try to improve the state marketing
system. To make the state marketing system more concerned
with preserving the quality of agricultural products and more
adept at bridging the gap between producer and consumer is
the kind of goal that motivates Russia's decentralization of
responsibility and pursuit of profit.

   Looking at the farm unit itself, we see a need for a more
highly qualified administrative staff to be developed through
the decentralization reforms. If the farm's decision making
authority is to be expanded, then the farm officials must have
a type of training not necessary previously. Recognizing this,
Russia's political leaders and commentators have emphasized
strongly the need for increased numbers of specialists working in agriculture and for the development of local expertise
in decisions concerning the use of chemical fertilizers, irrigation and drainage facilities, and farm machinery and equipment. The following chapters refer frequently to this essential
part of the decentralization reforms.

   Decentralization of decision-making authority raises many
questions concerning the financing of investment. Clearly, if
decentralization is really to occur, then the central planners'
power over allocation of investment funds must be curtailed.

Yet, if such power were completely eliminated, then it is
feared that several new problems would likely arise. The
business cycle might reappear, with its inflation due to excessive aggregate demand and its unemployment arising when
aggregate demand is inadequate. In addition, a considerable
sphere of investment might be ignored by decentralized
decision makers because of a low rate of profit, and yet these
investments might be worthwhile from the view of the community or nation as a whole. The existence of external economies
or diseconomies could mean that the financial aspects considered by the local decision makers would not be the only
relevant considerations in regard to an investment: the impact
of one firm's investment decision on the economic activities
of other firms or individuals might also be important. Hence,
it is felt that some central controls must be retained.

With the decentralization reforms, Russia is entering a
new economic framework which presents its leaders with a
new set of economic problems and which requires a new set
of governmental techniques and policies for intervention in
the economy. The banking system, in particular, is acquiring
a new significance, and a question of major importance for
the government concerns the role the banks should play in the
future. The first part of this book raises such questions within
the context of the agricultural production process.

As already mentioned, it has not been a goal of this book
to present a complete account of the characteristics of Soviet
agriculture or of the events that have affected it. Rather, the
purpose has been to provide a unified set of examples of the
shortcomings that have arisen with the Stalin-Khrushchev
system of central planning and that underlie the Russian profit
reforms. I should emphasize that these shortcomings are
presented from the view of Russian political leaders and commentators. The reforms have been instituted because the
political leaders felt them to be necessary; the first part of
this book seeks to explain this desire for change. This approach relies upon few explicit comparisons between the
U.S.S.R. and other nations; rather it relies heavily upon
speeches and statements reported in the Russian press, especially during the few years preceding the reforms.

ALTERNATIVE APPROACHES TO
CENTRAL PLANNING

The second part of this book considers the profit reforms
in more general terms. It does so first within the context of

a broad discussion of government intervention in the economy. Here economic planning is viewed as a spectrum within which we can see many quite distinct frameworks for government intervention.   Three of these frameworks are examined in some detail: first, the centralization of all decisions concerning the operation of the economy; second, decentralized decision making, with guidelines such as centrally determined prices for each industry and each region; and third, decentralized decision making with prices competitively determined in the market and with the planning taking the form of aggregate monetary and fiscal policy.

In the first framework, with centralization of all decisions concerning economic activities, the planners are concerned with every detail in each enterprise. At least in theory, such a framework provides certainty concerning the path of economic events.   Ideally, it can avoid depression or inflation, and it can ensure that each sector develops in exactly the correct proportion to prevent shortages or excesses of any commodity. The prevision promised by such a framework of economic planning is indeed appealing. Yet, in practice, such precision may not be achieved. Shortcomings may arise in the conveying of accurate and appropriate information from each enterprise to the central planners, in the coordination of all production and consumption plans, and in the flexibility required whenever changes in production or consumption conditions occur. In the modern economy, the increasing importance of quality and technological progress have compounded these shortcomings to the extent that this first framework has lost much of the appeal it once had. This, of course, is the view supported in the first part of this book.

The third framework involves the kind of central planning practiced by Western nations with such techniques as monetary, fiscal, and tariff policies. Here the goals being pursued have concerned national aspects of economic activity. In particular, these governments have sought to avoid economic depressions on the one hand, and inflation on the other. Many have attempted to expand their manufacturing sector, or at least prevent its contraction, by erection of tariff barriers against imports. Here the central planners are not concerned with every detail in each enterprise, nor even with details in each type of industry or in each region of the country; rather, they are concerned with aggregate information. They are seeking to affect the total level of economic activity in their nation or the total level of manufacturing as a whole. There is one taxation policy for the nation--it is not differentiated by industry or

by region. Similarly, there is one monetary policy, and there
may be one tariff policy.

This third framework has a variety of shortcomings. As
already mentioned, private decision makers may ignore the
impact of their decisions on the economic activities of other
firms or individuals. External economies may be disregarded,
so that an industry may receive less investment than it should.
Transportation and communication systems, education and
research, or basic industries like steel and chemicals may
require special government assistance if they are to develop;
yet their expansion may have stimulating repercussions
throughout the economy. External diseconomies may be disregarded, so that other firms or individuals are harmed by
one industry's expansion. This is the case, for example,
with the various types of pollution. Such externalities do not
require detailed supervision of all aspects of each firm's
economic activities. They may require special government
policies for particular industries.

Uniform monetary and fiscal policies do not affect all
industries, geographic regions, or socioeconomic classes
equally. A policy of tight money and increased levels of
taxation, aimed at reducing inflation, may raise unemployment levels and restrain incomes disproportionately in depressed economic regions, city slums, and low-income
groups. They may hamstring the housing industry and hurt
those individuals connected with construction to a far greater
extent than those employed in other industries. On the other
hand, national policies to stimulate growth may be unable to
affect the pockets of poverty that have persisted in many of
the economically advanced Western nations.

Lack of government intervention in specific industries
may lead, in some cases, to a collusion among producers.
Oligopoly or monopolistic competition may result in price
increases and market distortions; monopolies may create
similar effects. The public, as consumers, may be hurt by
such developments.

Until the 1960's, the U.S.S.R. adhered basically to the
first framework while Western nations adhered basically to
the third framework. So long as this was the case, meaningful
or useful comparisons of central planning were severely
limited. The topic of "comparative economic systems" has,
to a major degree, been a misnomer. In general, during
peacetime, the kinds of economic problems attacked by central planners, the techniques and policies used, and the information and analyses required for planning have differed so
radically between the U.S.S.R. on the one hand, and Western

nations on the other, that neither Russians nor Westerners could benefit from a better knowledge of the other's experience. Wartime mobilizations, when Western governments have sought to coordinate production plans of all enterprises connected with defense industries, have perhaps been an exception.

The profit reforms and Russian discussions concerning them have dealt with a planning framework somewhere between the two just described. Decision-making authority is decentralized, and profit maximization is to be an important guide for local decision makers. Each economic enterprise is to have considerable freedom in regard to the raw materials and machinery it is to purchase, the commodities it is to produce, the production methods it is to use, and the customers to whom it is to sell its output. Central planners are not to be involved in each firm's operations in the way they were formerly. In this regard, the second framework resembles the third. Yet central planners will be concerned with each industry and with each region of the country. Planners, for example, will be responsible for setting prices, including the rate of interest. Within any one industry and region, the economic enterprises will face the same set of prices and other guidelines; yet such prices and guidelines may differ greatly from one industry or region to another. Here the rejection of a single set of economic policies for the entire nation and the need for disaggregated data and analysis, on which to base differentiated policies, resembles the first framework.

Lying between the first and third types of economic planning, this second framework is largely unexplored. Relatively little has been written concerning the probable behavior of enterprises operating within the context of such centrally determined guidelines; and hence relatively little is known concerning the advantages and disadvantages of various possible types of guidelines. Yet it is my contention that this second framework may become increasingly important in both Western and Communist nations. The Russian reforms actually instituted to the present date have merely ventured onto this unexplored terrain. Western experiments with regional development policies, urban renewal programs, pollution controls, and other practices that have sought to combine central guidelines with decentralized initiative and responsibility represent significant steps into the same area.

The latter part of this book seeks to investigate the second framework for government intervention in the economy. This is certainly not a complete investigation. Many interesting and important aspects are not analyzed thoroughly. In fact, one of my key arguments is that some relevant questions cannot be answered on the basis of theoretical analysis alone; only actual experience can indicate which of several paths is best to follow. Clearly this is not a definitive work; rather it is a call for further exploration of an extremely important but hitherto neglected economic subject. Such additional investigation can be meaningful for both Russian and Western economic planners. With the analysis of the second framework for government intervention, the study of comparative economic systems can attain a new significance. Conclusions derived from the study of Soviet experience in this area will be of interest not solely for the specialist in Soviet events but rather for the economist, regardless of his particular specialty.

I should mention that, in the view of the Soviet and Western economic systems presented above, the question of private versus public ownership is largely ignored, as are the moral or ethical connotations that it arouses. Rather, what I have presented is a definition of the economic system that is based only upon the type of central planning practiced by the government. Hence, my view of the convergence of the Soviet and Western economic systems does not take such factors as income differentials or attitudes towards private property into account. It is simply the view of an economist who has considered techniques and policies for economic planning and has recognized that, in the future, meaningful comparisons may be drawn between Russia and the West. Each will be able to learn from the other's experience.

The 1960's have witnessed vigorous debates within the U.S.S.R. concerning various aspects of the decentralization reforms, and a considerable literature now exists on the opinions of Soviet political leaders and economists. The second part of this book presents a summary and interpretation of such views as a background against which a theoretical analysis of several aspects of the reforms is presented.

DECENTRALIZED DECISION MAKING

The Stalin-Khrushchev system of detailed central planning did not, in fact, eliminate all decision-making power at the enterprise level. As the first part of this book indicates, enterprises have consciously acted in ways that Soviet leaders have criticized. Enterprises, for example, have consciously

produced inferior or inappropriate goods or have failed to
meet specified delivery dates. This is partially due to the
fact that the problems of information, coordination, and
flexibility have prevented the central planners from setting
meaningful quality standards for each product. It is also due
to the failure of supervisory controls over quality and the
failure of the incentive system to foster local concern for
quality. Neither external controls nor internal incentives
have motivated enterprise management to make the desired
decisions when they have power to do so. Producers seeking
only to maximize gross output have felt little concern for the
needs and desires of their customers in regard to quality, or
for innovations that will reduce production costs. Customers,
on the other hand, have been restricted in their ability to turn
to alternative sources of supply. If the sphere of enterprise
power and influence is to be expanded, it is clear that the set
of guidelines and incentives, in accordance with which enterprises have made decisions in the past, must be reformed.
To leave the previous set of guidelines and incentives intact
could result in a devastating extension of the malpractices
already common under the Stalin-Khrushchev system.

One approach might be to have each firm maximize its
total profits and provide bonuses on this basis. This approach
has shortcomings, however. The Russians realize that everyone is not equally endowed with ability and initiative and,
therefore, that the question of promotions or demotions is
extremely important. Can total profits serve as a satisfactory
index in deciding this issue? The answer may be negative,
quite apart from the sensitivity of profits to prices. Some
firms are much larger than others and could be expected to
enjoy a much larger profit. In spite of a small total profit
figure, the manager of a small firm may be doing a better
job than the manager of a larger firm with its larger total
profit. If the smaller firm's manager had access to all the
capital he wished to borrow, and if he faced an infinite lifetime, then the smaller firm could be expanded to the full
capacity of the manager's ability and initiative. The economy
would suffer a loss due to the manager's lower productivity
during the time he worked with a smaller enterprise than his
ability and initiative warranted, but the total of such losses
might not be considered excessive. The brevity of a manager's
lifetime and the fact that expansion of a firm is hampered by
institutional barriers combine to make job promotion or de-
motion extremely important for the economy's success. This
is true, as well, of promotions within the branches or departments of a firm.

Success in the system of promotions and demotions argues
against reliance on an index of total profits. Equity in the
system of bonuses also argues against total profits. The
manager of the smaller firm who is doing a better job than the
manager of the larger firm should, perhaps, receive a larger
bonus in spite of his firm's smaller total profits. From this
viewpoint, the amount of profits per unit of capital might be
a more appropriate index of management success. Or the
volume of profit per worker might be more equitable, especially for a system of cooperatives or collective farms. Such
alternative gauges of success may lead to distortions in production methods, however. The manager seeking to maximize
profits per unit of capital or of labor may alter the capital or
labor intensity of his firm in a manner that reduces efficiency
but improves his success indicator. What will be the extent
of this reduction in efficiency? The answer to this question
will depend upon the technical aspects of the production
process, such as the ease with which input substitutions can
be made and the specific nature of the cost functions faced by
the firm. Hence theoretical analysis alone cannot provide a
complete understanding of this problem; and even conclusions
based upon actual enterprise experience may vary over time
as new technology alters the production or cost functions upon
which management decisions are based.

The Russian decentralization reforms actually instituted
have not placed sole reliance upon the maximization of some
aspect of profit. They have also included sales maximization
as a success indicator. The relative advantages of these
criteria deserve examination. We will investigate this
question, in particular, in regard to the implications of price
lags. As demand for a commodity changes, or, as new technology is developed, the optimal price for that commodity
varies. It is reasonable to assume that some time may
elapse between the change in demand or technology and the
alteration, by the central planners, of relative prices. What
happens to the quality of the particular commodity and to
cost-reducing innovation in its production during such price
lags may be of major importance in deciding upon the practical desirability of this central-planning framework.

With this centralized determination of prices, local decisions concerning product quality may take on a variety of
new and significant characteristics. Monopolistic or oligopolistic behavior may appear, for example. Here agreements
to reduce product quality may resemble the collusion to increase prices within Western nations. Or oligopolistic and

monopolistic competition may result in quality fluctuations that are similar to the price wars of Western enterprises. A considerable body of economic literature has been developed in regard to monopoly, oligopoly, and monopolistic competition in the Western context of our third planning framework. With the focus shifted from price formation to determination of quality, this literature becomes relevant for the second framework into which the U.S.S.R. is now venturing.

The differential pricing policies instituted in the U.S.S.R. promise higher prices for high-cost producers than they do for low-cost producers. On the surface, this would seem to foster inefficient and high-cost production. The Soviet approach is based, however, on a faith in the potential for economic development. It is thought that backward regions should be encouraged to expand their economic activities, and that through such expansion these regions will adopt the modern efficiency that will reduce their costs.

Whether this second framework will, in general, be superior to the Stalin-Khrushchev planning system is a question that only future experience can answer. Similarly, we cannot be sure of the relative advantage of the second framework compared with the government intervention previously practiced in Western nations. As time passes, future innovations in computer machinery and techniques may further complicate our evaluations by altering the relative advantages of the different planning systems. What is clear is that dissatisfaction with past experience has been sufficient to warrant experimentation with a new type of planning framework and that the results of such experimentation deserve close scrutiny by citizens of both Russia and the West.

NOTES

1.   A. N. Kosygin, "On Improving the Management of Industry," Pravda (September 28, 1965), pp. 1-4, as translated in the Current Digest of the Soviet Press, XVII, 38 (1965), 3-12.

2.   CPSU Central Committee, Pravda (February 16, 1964), pp. 1-2; as translated in the Current Digest of the Soviet Press, XVI, 8 (1964), 1-2.

3.   L. I. Brezhnev, "Land Reclamation Is a Fundamental Problem," Pravda (May 28, 1966), pp. 1-2.

CHAPTER **2** THE CHEMICAL
FERTILIZER INDUSTRY

INTRODUCTION

Prior to 1928 neither private enterprise on the one hand, nor the governments of Tsarist Russia or the U.S.S.R. on the other, undertook any significant development of a chemical-fertilizer industry. In 1913, domestic production was greatly exceeded by the importation of about 260,000 tons of phosphorous and superphosphate fertilizers as well as some nitrogen and potassium fertilizers. In the decade following the revolution, domestic production rose (from a total of 65,000 tons in 1913 to 208,000 tons in 1929). Imports of fertilizers fell substantially, however, with the result that " . . . one thing cannot be doubted: in 1929 the Soviet Union used even less mineral fertilizer than Russia in 1913."[1] Table 1 presents production data for two types of fertilizers, nitrogen and superphosphate, for selected years from 1913 to 1934.

In 1928 a new attitude towards mineral fertilizers suddenly appeared in party and government declarations. An official resolution "concerning measures for raising crop yields" emphasized "the decisive significance of the application of mineral fertilizer for raising crop yields."[2] Several industrial complexes were constructed for its production, and previously existing factories were expanded. Domestic production before 1928 had been based nearly entirely on imported raw materials. Henceforth the natural resources of the U.S.S.R. itself were to be utilized. The locations of these enterprises now were to be determined with a view towards the geographical pattern of natural resources, rather than being built, as previously, in the port cities. Hence in several areas complete settlements,

---

The material in this chapter was summarized in the author's article, "Barriers to Technological Change in the U.S.S.R.: A Study of Chemical Fertilizers," Soviet Studies, XX, 3, January, 1969.

20

providing for social overhead capital as well as mines and factories, had to be established. This latter consideration meant that expansion of the fertilizer industry presented complex problems in the sphere of coordination among various economic sectors.

TABLE 1

Manufacture of Nitrogen and Superphosphate
Fertilizers in U.S.S.R. (in Tons) 1913,
1928, 1930-1934

Year	Nitrogen	Superphosphate
1913	13,800	21,400
1928	11,200	184,771
1930	------	391,836
1931	27,500	518,787
1932	55,600	615,649
1933	110,900	690,204
1934	226,000	1,163,950

Source: V. C. Lelchuk, The Creation of the Chemical Industry of the U.S.S.R. (Moscow: Nauka, 1964) pp. 234 and 272.

TABLE 2

Implementation of Investment Plans in Seventeen
Soviet Chemical Plants, 1929-1930

	Implemented in 11 Months (thousand rubles)	Portion Implemented of Plan in 11 Months (per cent)
New construction	82,856	52.2
Expansion and reconstruction	46,819	74.7
Capital repairs	5,183	87.8

Source: V. C. Lelchuk, The Creation of the Chemical Industry of the U.S.S.R. (Moscow: Nauka, 1964), p. 185.

Table 2 indicates that nearly two-thirds of investment in seventeen chemical plants over an eleven-month period consisted of entirely new construction. No data relate specifically to fertilizer plants, but this proportion no doubt was higher because of the near absence of prior factories, the rapid construction of new plants, and the fact that several of the latter were built in previously unsettled areas in order to be near sources of raw materials. It is important to note that plan implementation in construction of such new projects was frustrated to a considerably greater extent than plan implementation dealing with expansion and reconstruction of already existing plants or dealing with capital repairs. V. C. Lelchuk's description of each fertilizer project reveals the common difficulty of practical coordination when the area concerned lacked any prior industrial structure.

The first potassium mine in the U.S.S.R. was built at Solikamsk in the Urals. By the end of 1932 less than 25 per cent of the living area needed by the personnel had been constructed, with the result that inability to attract and retain a labor force was a major problem. Lack of a railway branch-line compounded supply problems. In 1929, work was begun on the development of phosphorous mines in the Khibian Peninsula. Here "38.7 per cent of all annual investment went for constructing living premises; and, in spite of this high proportion of investment, the problem of living accommodations was solved slowly."[3] For production of nitrogen fertilizers, a plant was built at Bobriki, as part of an entirely new city in the coal-basin region below Moscow. Another plant was constructed in the previously existing city of Berezniki in the Urals. Yet even here the labor force was not willing to commit itself entirely to the new industry. "Eighty per cent of all (industrial) workers were connected with agriculture . . . and about two-thirds had cows and were occupied with haymaking."[4] In the early stages of construction, monthly departures of workers totalled over one-half of monthly arrivals. At Chernoresh, on the other hand, a factory that produced nitrogen fertilizer already existed. Lelchuk emphasizes that a skilled labor force with knowledge and experience in this industrial sector resulted in a more rapid rate of progress and, in fact, the nature of its performance was entirely different from that developing in Bobriki and Berezniki.

In 1938 the Eighteenth Congress CPSU proclaimed the third five-year plan to be the Five Years for Chemistry and it planned a further program of construction of chemical fertilizer factories.[5]

Redirection of the economy towards production for war purposes prevented any extensive expansion, however, and reconstruction of plant and equipment physically destroyed required several post-war years. It was not until the 1950's that another major advance occurred in this sector. Once more, raw-material sources not previously utilized were opened up. This expansion in several cases again entailed development of completely new settlements with a need for social overhead capital and for a meshing of the time patterns of numerous economic activities. It is with the latter period that this chapter is concerned; and here we shall focus on the inability to achieve a satisfactory transformation in regard to quality appropriateness, and production techniques in general.

In the Soviet press, nearly every article concerning chemical fertilizer mentions three shortcomings. Fertilizers are not processed in such a way as to prevent deterioration in the time interval between production and use. Fertilizers are not concentrated so as to reduce costs of transportation and application; that is, useless ballast makes up more of their weight and volume than is necessary. Production of compound fertilizers--containing nitrogen, phosphorous, and potassium--instead of merely one of these nutrients--is too small.[6] In February, 1966, the Twenty-third Congress of the CPSU resolved:

To increase significantly the production of concentrated and complex mineral fertilizers. Toward the
end of the five years to turn out fertilizers only in
granulated and non-caking forms.

To improve significantly the quality of fertilizer.
To provide for the utilization of mineral fertilizer in
the kolkhozy and sovkhozy on a scientific basis. To
take measures towards a sharp reduction in the loss
of fertilizer during its transportation and storage.[7]

In April 1966, Kosygin stated:

The chemical industry will increase its output of
mineral fertilizers every year; deliveries will
double. Parallel with an increase in the production
of fertilizers as an urgent task is a rise in their
quality and the elimination of losses through transportation, storage, and utilization.[8]

To improve the quality of a product is not necessarily an advisable policy. The benefits received from a quality improvement must be weighed against the costs incurred in implementing the improvement. In the following discussion of the chemical fertilizer industry, we shall assume that adoption of quality improvements is economically advisable.

A precise analysis of this assumption would be interesting but,
unfortunately, the author does not possess the data necessary
for such an analysis. In any case, for our purposes we do
not require the strong assumption of economic advisability--
only the assumption that Soviet party and government officials
have believed quality improvements to be advisable. As already mentioned, a major focus of our discussion will be the
hypothesis that obstacles prevent Soviet firms from imme-
diately adopting modern technology, that these obstacles arise
because of the planning and administrative framework within
which Soviet industry operates, and that changes in this framework are necessary if the obstacles are to be removed. To
discuss this hypothesis, we require only the assumption that
a rational rejection of the modern technology on the grounds
of its costs is not the real reason for the current situation.
Frequent references will be made to remarks of party
and administration officials in order to illustrate that such
rational rejection is not the case.

A speech by Khrushchev in 1958 indicated several of the
weaknesses that will be explored in this chapter. In his speech,
Khrushchev made the following series of comments:

> The existence of serious shortcomings in the organ-
> ization of research in the field of synthetic materials
> is one of the main reasons for the lag in the develop-
> ment of new branches of the chemical industry . . .
> The main reason for the lag in this field of science
> and technology lies in serious imperfections in the
> organization of research and experimental work . . .
> Some institutions and scientists work in isolation
> from the needs of industry and give the country
> nothing year after year . . . The Ministry of the
> Chemical Industry pays little attention to the work
> of the scientific institutes, does not check to see if
> major assignments are carried out, and does not
> give the institutes the help they need . . . It must
> be said that the U.S.S.R. Academy of Sciences has
> also paid extremely insufficient attention to the
> scientific problems involved in producing and using
> synthetic materials. [9]

These are indeed harsh words for the scientific research
institutes. Why did they tend to "work in isolation from the
needs of industry?" This question deserves further examination.

> Successful development of the chemical industry re-
> quires that many new designs of equipment be de-
> veloped and introduced in production as soon as
> possible. [10]

We shall discuss the organization of the Soviet design institutes and shall consider the extent to which their functioning facilitates innovation--the implementation of scientific advances in the actual production process and the adaptation or improvement of already existing techniques to reduce costs or raise the quality of the product. Have these institutes provided the equipment designs necessary for the manufacture of new types of chemical fertilizers? Have they responded to the demands of the fertilizer plants for certain modifications and improvements?

It should be said that in the past the chemical equipment produced by the machine-building industry was in many cases technically inferior to the best foreign models . . . In order to carry out the extensive program for the construction and prompt commissioning of chemical enterprises for the production and processing of synthetic materials, we must increase the output of chemical, technological, and auxiliary equipment more than three-fold by 1965 in comparison with 1957 . . . The production base of enterprises producing equipment for the chemical industry should be greatly expanded. [11]

Why has chemical equipment tended to be "technically inferior?" Here our discussion will focus on the links between the machine-building industry and the scientific and design institutes on the one hand, and between the machine-building industry and the chemical fertilizer plants on the other.

An incorrect technical policy pursued for a long time by the Ministry of the Chemical Industry impeded the development of synthetic materials production in our country . . . The planning agencies and the Ministry of Chemical Industry did not allocate sufficient capital funds for the development of new branches of the chemical industry, and what funds were allocated were used very unsatisfactorily . . . One reason for the lag in the development of these industries is that the Ministry of the Chemical Industry and the former Ministry of the Oil Industry underestimated the use of oil gases and natural gases as the most accessible and cheapest raw material for the production of synthetic materials. [12]

Here Krushchev has emphasized a most important problem in the inertia of the officials in the regular government administration--an inertia which might prevent the introduction of many constructive changes in types of products or in methods of production and utilization. This question will be discussed in more detail and arguments will be presented concerning the advisability of decentralized decision making to permit a flexibility and adaptability that has been lacking in the traditional planning and administrative framework.

SCIENTIFIC RESEARCH

Two distinct types of scientific research institutions exist side by side in the Soviet Union. The work of the <u>academic institutes</u>, affiliated to the republic or U.S.S.R. Academies of Science, is basically theoretical. The work of the <u>branch institutes</u>--which are affiliated to some specific industry and are subordinate, just as any ordinary factory is, to the regular administrative hierarchy--exhibits a strong applied-science inclination.

Historically, a situation has developed wherein the academic institutes are responsible to the state for the preparation of the new theoretical basis of the sciences, while the institutes in the branches of the national economy are responsible for preparing new types of production. The cadres, the specific methods of experimentation, and also the auxiliary base of the institutes have been formed in accordance with this. [13]

Of considerable importance is the question of cooperation between these two kinds of research institutes. Such cooperation should foster the efficient transmission to applied research of any gains made in theoretical work and also the theoretical analysis of mistakes and difficulties encountered in the development and mastery of new engineering methods. The bureaucratic apparatus of any given branch of industry is better able to organize the planned, nationwide dissemination of scientific advances than is any single academic institute which lacks such comprehensive contacts with the industrial enterprises. Intimate cooperation between the two types of institutes appears essential for the successful operation of each. "Unfortunately," however, "the chemical institutes of the Academy of Sciences still have only feeble contacts with the branch institutes of the chemical industry and even weaker contacts with the research laboratories of the large chemical combines."[14] Since 1963 some provisions have been established for the directors of the academic institutes to report to the State Committee of the Petroleum and Chemical

Industry on the orientation of current research projects and
plans for future projects in their respective institutes. Soviet
authorities hope that this will expand the scale of industrial
application of scientific advances. [15]

As another aspect of this problem, it is frequently suggested that the chemical institutes stand in need of pilot-plant
bases. [16] These pilot plants should consist of complexes of
small-scale installations which can be rearranged easily to
simulate numerous productive processes on a scale larger
than that permitted by the laboratory. Such a strengthening
of the experimental base is seen as a concrete means of increasing the practical applicability of advances made by the
scientific institutes, both academic and branch. In his discussion of "Obstacles to the Introduction of the Attainments
of Chemical Science into Industry, " M. Koton notes that "in
the planning and economic organizations, all are agreed that
without a broad laboratory and realistic experimental base in
the scientific research institutes and large plants it is impossible to realize rapidly the attainments of science in the
chemical industry. " Yet what must be done in order to build
the necessary pilot plants and small-scale multipurpose industrial equipment?

It is a matter of separating that branch of machine
building which would be completely specialized on
the development and manufacture of laboratory and
experimental equipment . . . Special experimental
design offices would have to be added to these particular instrument and machine-building plants.
Their sole purpose would be to serve the needs of
the chemical institutes and other scientific organizations. [17]

Hence, to improve the effectiveness of scientific research,
even the machine-building industry must be altered in a significant manner.

In February, 1964, at the Plenary Session of the Central
Committee of the CPSU, Khrushchev discussed the scientific
research institutes. Nearly six years had passed since his
1958 speech in which, before the same body, he had criticized
vigorously the organization of research and the tendency for
"some institutions and scientists to work in isolation from the
needs of industry. "[18] His words now were:

It is apparent that we must have some kind of agency
to deal with major scientific-economic problems.
We must so arrange matters that we not only notice
promptly all the best and most progressive achievements science offers and not only give impetus to
major scientific discoveries and inventions but, in

addition, foresee the importance for the national
economy as a whole of this or that new trend in
science; that is, we must determine promptly not
only its scientific and technological but also its
political and economic importance. [19]

This time Khrushchev attacked a slightly different aspect
of the same basic problem--the relation between science and
industry. Already by 1962, twenty-eight new institutes had
been established and many new affiliates and laboratories had
been created since 1958; the number of scientific workers in
chemistry had increased by almost 150 per cent; appropria-
tions for chemical science had risen by 250 per cent. Much
more was being achieved by the scientific institutes than had
been achieved prior to 1958. The rate of scientific advance
had been augmented considerably. Yet still the chemical industry was not benefiting as fully as government officials had
expected. We might well wonder whether the creation of one
more organization, as Khrushchev suggested, could remove
this obstacle to technological progress.

A 1965 article by E. Aliyeva, "Why New Petrochemical
Processes Are Applied Slowly, "[20] examines this obstacle
between science and industry in greater detail. She notes
that frequently the introduction of an innovation has dragged
on for many years. Often when a process is being elaborated
the people in the institute take no account of the scale of production for which the process will be used. The scientists'
recommendations are often not sufficiently clear. Nevertheless, having completed the research and turned the results
over to the design organizations--the next stage of the journey
into production--the scientists consider their mission accom-
plished. They do not stop to consider whether the data which
they have furnished will satisfy the needs of the designers,
whether or not their suggestions are applicable in practice.
"The important thing to them is that one more planned research project has been completed. "[21] Hence it is sometimes
impossible, Aliyeva states, to construct designs for equipment based on the data provided by the scientific institutes.

"A process developed in the laboratory cannot travel to
industry by stages. The scientists must escort it in all
phases of its journey to the industrial enterprises. "[22] Aliyeva
states that officials of the republic Council of the National
Economy and of industrial enterprises and the representatives
of design organizations visit the scientific centers only rarely,
nor do the scientists visit the enterprises often. In order to
strengthen the ties between science and industry, this writer
suggests that each institute should have a material stake in the

utilization of innovations developed by its scientists. They
should be paid for their research only after the technological
processes, machines, and instruments born in their laboratories are being employed successfully in industry. This
desire to expand use of legal contracts binding two economic
entities--and perhaps negotiated by them independently of
central planners--has appeared many times in Soviet discussions.

Within the past few years an expansion has taken place
in structures which sometimes serve as alternatives to the
scientific research institutes--an expansion which has occurred
through the efforts of practical individuals somehow to overcome the obstacles between science and industry described in
the above comments. This development has not been ushered
into the economic scene with the fanfare characteristic of
many organizational changes; yet it could be of great practical
significance, and it does present an interesting facet of the
decentralization of decision-making debate.

A growth in the number and activity of government experimental farms has strengthened the links between science
and the chemical fertilizer industry, as well as between these
two spheres of activity and agriculture. The Belorussian
Academy of Agricultural Science, for example, has developed
the Ustye and Borovlyany Experimental Stations to test the
effectiveness of various fertilizer mixtures which its scientists
create. The Drabovskiy experimental field fulfills the same
function for the Ukrainian Scientific Research Institute of
Agriculture.[23] At such special farms, officials from ordinary
kolkhozy (collective or cooperative farms) and sovkhozy (state
farms) can see for themselves the benefits to be gained from
properly utilizing the chemical fertilizers which are now
becoming available in increasing quantities. Being intimately
connected with their parent research institute, such experimental stations also indicate to the scientists the limitations
of past efforts and can suggest future areas of research.

The universities are now attaining a prominent position in
this field of science. The Kharkov Polytechnical Institute
Imeni V. I. Lenin, for example, is conducting research concerning chemical fertilizers. Significant research was conducted by this university jointly with the State Institute of the
Nitrogen Industry and the Lisichansk Chemical Combine in
simplifying production of nitric acid and reducing its cost.
From these efforts, a new method has been developed for the
production of highly concentrated nitric acid. The Physio-
chemical Scientific Research Institute of Irkutsk University
has conducted experimental tests of fertilizers, and Tomsk

University has investigated new techniques for the production
of potash.

In recent years chemical combines have expanded their
own facilities for research and experimentation in an effort
to solve pressing scientific problems by themselves. Workers
at the Kemerovo Nitrogen Fertilizer Plant in the Kuznetsk
Basin, for example, have developed more active catalysts
than those previously used. The "GK-2 catalyst," produced
in collaboration with the Institute of the Nitrogen Industry, has
proven particularly useful. An investigation of a single-
stage method of producing ammonium nitrate has been conducted jointly with the institute, using a pilot plant at the
Kemerovo Combine.[24]

The Voskresensk Chemical Combine in Moskovskaya
oblast has also started organized research in chemical fertilizers. Jointly with staff members of the Scientific Research
Institute for Fertilizers it produced a triple superphosphate
in which the phosphorous content available to plants reaches
68 per cent. A special experimental shop was built in which
the manufacturing process for the production of this fertilizer
could be perfected.[25] At the Soligorsk Potassium Combine
in Byelorussia a laboratory has been built in which the
chemists together with factory workers can perform experiments. A pilot plant is also being planned for the concentration
of potassium salts by a method proposed by scientists at the
Soligorsk Combine in collaboration with the Institute of Chemistry of the Byelorussian Academy of Sciences.[26]

Occasionally writers have criticized this disorganized
proliferation of scientific organizations. Professor L. Kulikovsky has stated that in the Volga Valley there are now more
than 100 such organizations. They are subordinate, he claims,
to twenty-four different ministries, state committees, and
other departments. Many of them are affiliates of institutes
seated in Moscow. "No one in the economic region is concerned with planning and coordinating their activities; this
is done by various central agencies, through intricate, inter-
twining channels" with the result that such coordination is
"often useless."[27] Observers criticize the work of the
U.S.S.R. State Committee for the Coordinating of Scientific
Research and such criticism has become more vigorous as
these alternative research organizations have expanded their
activities. Three writers examining scientific research in
Siberia, for example, have claimed that "fertilizer research
at the institutes and scientific establishments of Siberia is
not coordinated, the staffs of the individual institutes mutually
duplicating their activities."[28]

A clear division of opinion is evident concerning this proliferation of uncoordinated research activities. On the one
hand, stand those who believe that what is needed is a perfecting of the present system of central coordination. Here can
be found writers who urge that the existing State Committee
for the Coordination of Scientific Research be given greater
powers and made more effective. More scientific conferences
and more visits by scientists to other research organizations
are also suggested. As noted above, Khrushchev in 1964
recommended the creation of a new agency to be entrusted
with the analysis, from the economic point of view, of all
major scientific discoveries and inventions. Several writers
have criticized severely the system of patents and have urged
that it be improved. Yu. Sergeyev and O. Tereshchenko have
stated that:

> Many scientific-technical organizations and enter-
> prises have long been engaged in working out new
> technology without knowing what has been achieved
> either in our own country or abroad . . . A well
> organized technological information service supply-
> ing patent information first and foremost can be of
> substantial assistance in this regard. [29]

B. Vasilyev claims that:

> The brief information on the content of patents that
> one finds in the All-Union Patent and Technical
> Library is insufficient for serious professional
> work . . . It would be advisable to set up a system
> of patent reproductions and to supply all large enter-
> prises and scientific institutions with reproduc-
> tions. [30]

It is true that such alterations, particularly in regard to
the patent system, might be of significant value. Certain
other writers, however, emphasize decentralization of responsibility for innovation as the key element necessary for
the major improvement that is desired. As noted above,
many Soviet commentators have stressed that at least a segment of the scientific community must become more intimately involved in the implementation of scientific discoveries,
and that it should be encouraged to do so by material rewards
geared to the final success of each particular venture. Once
scientists are linked with individual firms through such a
system of contracts, or through direct employment, decentralization of responsibility may provide not only a greater
flexibility in the pursuit of technological progress, but also,
accompanying the flexibility, an inevitably increasing lack of
coordination.

At the basis of this division of opinion, then, is the question of whether the benefits gained from the local initiative and independence will exceed those benefits that thorough centralized coordination could in practice achieve. The above discussion has presented harsh criticisms, by government officials, industrial workers, and economists, of the system of centralized coordination of scientific research and has noted a clear shift towards local initiative and independence. This seems to indicate that at the present time, if a final judgment in favor of decentralization in this sphere has not yet been made, at least the question of relative effectiveness is now being put to a test.

THE DESIGN INSTITUTES

The implementation of technological progress often requires the development and production of new types of machinery. For the manufacture of concentrated fertilizers, complex fertilizers and fertilizers which will not deteriorate while they are stored or transported, new equipment must be designed. In the U.S.S.R., the designing of plant and equipment is the task of a group of design institutes. Hence, these institutes play an important role in the adoption by industry of new chemical processes. We have seen that a basic problem in innovation is the strengthening of links between scientific research institutes and individual industrial enterprises. The design institutes face a similar problem.

> Shortcomings and miscalculations in design documentation cause enormous damage to the national economy . . . Last year (1963) an analysis was made of the nature of changes introduced in the technical documentation during the mastering of production of new items at a number of enterprises of the Volga Economic Region. About 60 per cent of the changes were caused by simple negligence on the part of designers, draftsmen, and other workers taking part in the preparation of the drawings. [31]

In many cases the design institutes are not aware of the precise needs of the relevant firms. Sometimes they seem to be simply uninterested in these needs; here we face the problem of appropriate incentive. In addition, we face the problem of links with science since the designers must be aware of the advances continually being achieved in that field. Once more we see the rise of alternative structures to fill the retarding

gap, particularly in the form of design departments within
individual chemical and machine-building enterprises.

In an article on "The Planning and Production of Chemical
Machines,"[32] A. Kuramzhin, director of one of the largest
chemical machine-building plants in the Soviet Union, has
noted that in recent years numerous modern materials such
as new acid-resistant types of steel, high-strength aluminum
alloys, special sections of rolled metal and pipes, and various
types of plastics have come into prominence in construction
and machine building. He claims that the design institutes
have made wide use of these materials in their drawings.
However, the construction trusts and machine builders are
often unable to obtain supplies of the type of material recommended. Thus the designers must not only possess a working
knowledge of these new substances; when drawing plans for a
plant they must also know whether that particular plant will
in fact be able to obtain the kind of material upon which their
designs are based.

V. Krotov, former Chairman of the Central Urals
Sovnarkhoz, has noted that the seven chemical machine-
building enterprises of his sovnarkhoz received plans and
designs from more than sixty institutes and organizations.[33]
Such a situation can easily lead to confusion in the factories
which receive the plans. Depending on the design institutes,
industrial firms lack individuals in their own employ capable
of remedying confusion; and the relevant institutes may be
located too far from the scene to be of ready service if an
emergency should arise.

Events at the Dneprodzerzhinsk Nitrogen Fertilizer Plant
illustrate another difficulty. Here the Dneprokhimstroy Trust,
in charge of the construction of the new enterprise, progressed
at a faster pace in its work than had been anticipated. Repeatedly, it had to reduce the number of workers on the project
because the design institutes were slow in providing the necessary plans. In one case it completed a shop for the manufacture of nitric acid only to be called back twice to effect
major revisions of the original plan. The basic instructions
in regard to the nitric acid shop had called for complete auto-
mation of production. However, the designers wished to cut
their planning costs. And so, rather than develop the required
changes in the production processes, they simply overlooked
the command to mechanize and automate. In the end, workers
still had to fill vessels with nitric acid manually.[34]

With such projects, we see the importance of both timing
and accuracy on the part of the designers.[35] These features

have become vexing problems because of the lack of regular
contacts between the design institutes on the one hand, and
the construction trusts and industrial enterprises on the other.
Repeatedly we encounter examples of workers waiting for
plans and then of the plans not being appropriate. The
Dneprodzerzhinsk project also indicates the importance of
the incentive problem with regard to the design institutes.
As with scientific-research institutes, the incomes of the designers and the funds available to any particular institute have
not depended on the extent to which they have provided concrete aid to industry. Here Soviet leaders face another
economic endeavor where the Stalin-Khrushchev system of
planning has not provided relevant success indicators. The
success-indicator problem has been deeply embedded in the
Soviet system and appears to have hindered progress in many
sectors of the economy. With regard to the scientific research institutes and the design institutes, the situation seems
particularly unfortunate.

That a negligent attitude on the part of the design institutes
can cause repercussions of an extremely serious nature can
be seen by considering a few actual situations. At the
Sredneuralsk Copper Smelting Plant the planners erred in
their blueprints dealing with the production of sulphuric acid
as a byproduct of the copper smelting process. As a result,
it was necessary to make alterations throughout the plant
which cost about 1 million rubles.[36] Designers in the
Mekhanobr Institute of the State Committee for Ferrous and
Non-Ferrous Metallurgy inaccurately calculated the amount
of water necessary in the operations of the Maardu Combine
in Estonia.[37] As a result, the latter firm was unable for
over a year to meet its planned figures for output of phosphor-
ite meal.

In an article dealing with "Problems in Supplying the
Chemical Industry with Machinery and Equipment,"[38] L. Glikman has described the development of equipment to produce
ammophos, a new fertilizer which contains nitrogen and
phosphorous and is of a highly concentrated nature. In spite
of the fact that this was a new product, each of the three design institutes involved developed its recommendations for
the creation of equipment without industrial testing. The cor-
rosion resistance of the metal used in the manufacture of a
spray dryer for processing the planned output was not carefully investigated. Even after the start-up of production, it
was necessary, states Glikman, to investigate anew the
properties of the materials and to seek other materials that

were more durable. He has criticized strenuously the weakness of the experimental base in this regard and has urged that it be improved. The Dzhambul Superphosphate Plant in Kazakhstan was the first enterprise to organize production of ammophos. It was supposed to start production in August of 1962. Yet a full year later only one-tenth of the designed productive capacity had been achieved. The metal spray disk for drying the fertilizer simply broke down after a few hours of operation. Suggestions by the Moscow design office were sent to the faraway plant in Kazakhstan, but the difficulties persisted. Finally, the plant's own workers developed a type of spray nozzle which served the purpose, although even this was not successful enough to permit the other equipment to operate at full speed. [39]

"Quite often it happens that a newly opened enterprise operates on one-half or even one-fourth of its capacity for the first or even second year of its existence." [40] In explaining why this is so, V. Parfenov emphasizes the lack of experimentation on the part of the design institutes. The Shchekino Chemical Combine in Tul'skaya oblast, with its production of carbamide faced a situation to that of the Dzhambul Plant mentioned above. In this case, a pilot plant had been constructed to test the apparatus, but it had been operated for only one month. The Novomoskovsk Plant, located in the same oblast and responsible for this testing, explained that it was under pressure to fulfill the quota which it had been allocated and hence had no time to organize extensive experiments. [41]

Of the sixty models of new equipment built over a three-year period at the Bolshevik Plant, only thirty were tested before being mass produced. Why should any chemical enterprise move skilled workers from its regular production lines to man pilot equipment when such an action would risk possible bonuses, based on the plant's quantitative output, for the firm's staff? In order to receive a bonus for such experimental testing of new equipment, the plant must include the subject in a plan of scientific research work in August or September of the year prior to the actual testing. The design institutes, however, cannot postpone a project for what may be longer than a year, and so they seek in vain for a plant which will conscientiously perform their testing on short notice.

The Chardzhou Superphosphate Plant in Turkmenia started production in 1960. The aluminum fluoride division in this plant still was not engaged in actual production one and a half

years after it had been put into operation--because of the
errors in this project which had been drafted by the Giprokhim
Institute. Perhaps because of such an unpleasant experience,
the Chardzhou officials undertook to train workers in the field
of technology. They developed a cadre of highly skilled workers which began to study scientific advances and the practices
of the nation's leading chemical enterprises. Several other
chemical and machine-building enterprises have created their
own force of designers, so that the plant will not be compelled
to rely so heavily on outsiders for whom the success of any
particular plant is unimportant. Loyalty to one's fellow
workers, proximity to the difficulties as they arise, and a
greater willingness to experiment when one's own plant will
be the beneficiary of success, all tend to make the local
firm's designers of positive assistance.

An interesting article on this subject[42] has urged that for
new machinery and equipment the necessary scientific research, design and testing, and installation and improvement
should all be performed within each of the large industrial
firms. At present, however, a considerable obstacle to
complete self-reliance in this sphere is a lack of highly qualified scientists and designers in the employ of the individual
firms.

> A substantial segment of scientists should work
> directly in industry. But in practice there are now
> practically no specialists of higher qualifications
> (candidates and doctors of science) to be found in
> the plant laboratories and shops. All chemical
> scientists, as a rule, are on the staffs of the re-
> search institutes. The minute an engineer engaged
> in production defends his dissertation, he transfers
> to a research institute. [43]

Greater freedom concerning employment and pay rates must
be given each firm if this practice is to be reversed. The
author of the above quotation notes that in the German Democratic Republic the major shops and plant laboratories at
chemical firms are headed by scientists, and he claims that
because of this the innovation process seems to have functioned
more smoothly in that country than in the U.S.S.R.

At present, chemical firms lack a top group of formally
trained scientists; and because of this, current efforts within
each enterprise are mostly restricted to minor improvements.
Even these have sometimes been of significant value, and
they do provide indications of the shift that is occurring in
this sphere. Workers at the Ufa Chemical Combine have
aided their enterprise in numerous ways. Chlorine, for

example, had become a raw material whose supply was critically limited. The greatest bottleneck in the relevant shop was the electrolysis section which the Ufa chemists redesigned to increase capacity by 14 per cent. The Novomoskovsk Chemical Combine, one of the original Soviet fertilizer plants, was completely renovated in the late 1950's. One of the new products which it was to manufacture was carbamide. The Lisichansk and Shchekinsky Chemical Combines had already undertaken production of carbamide. Hence the workers of the Novomoskovsk firm examined the facilities of these other enterprises and managed to devise a new method of installing equipment and situating it in open premises. Along with other improvements, this reduced construction costs and enabled completion one year ahead of schedule. Since 1958 this plant has considered an average of 3,000 proposals for improvement per year, providing an average annual saving of about 1 million rubles. Novomoskovsk in Tul'skaya oblast opened the first shop in the nation for the production of simazin, a new herbicide. Here a bottleneck soon developed in the filtration and drying department. A group of employees was able to devise a system of drying racks which proved to be a significant advancement. The Rustavi Nitrogen Fertilizer Plant also has achieved success in creating an indigenous source of new production ideas. In the ammonium nitrate shop, for example, granulation towers had to be cleaned periodically since ammonium nitrate would adhere to their inside walls. At first this work was done manually and required four or five days. After application of a device suggested by the technical instructor at the shop, this task could now be performed in eight hours. Output could therefore be increased.

Some individuals, recognizing the trend for enterprises to develop their own design organizations and appreciating the value of this approach have suggested a major revision of that part of the economic system which we have so far examined. They have recommended that scientific and design institutes be amalgamated, in some cases, with machine-building firms to form a number of compact groups, each group being capable of organizing all the complex processes of equipping a new plant--from preparation of technical designs to starting up of production and mastery of operation of the equipment. Perhaps each group could contain several machine-building firms, so that it would be able to supply all the needs of any particular chemical plant. This suggestion possesses the great advantage that it fixes much more definitely the responsibility for inferior conduct. Under the

present system it is too easy to shift the blame; and the inter-
mingling of various organizations working on the same project
builds a smokescreen through which government officials cannot penetrate in order to inflict penalties on the laggards.   In
his report to the Supreme Soviet in 1964, Kosygin discussed
the need to reduce the length of time between the official open-
ing of a new enterprise and the attainment by that enterprise
of its designed capacity.   He emphasized that "the design
organizations should bear responsiblity for the quality of designs."[44] Decentralization of responsibility, in one form or
another, has been suggested by many observers of this problem.   It cannot be denied that here, as in the case of the
scientific research institutes, major flaws have existed along
the road which leads to an increase in the amount and effectiveness of chemical fertilizers and a decrease in the cost of
their production.

THE CHEMICAL MACHINE-
BUILDING INDUSTRY

From what we have already discussed, it is clear that
the tasks of every machine-building firm are made more
difficult by improper actions performed outside its own factory
walls.   We shall now consider several other ways in which
organizations beyond the control of the individual machine-
building enterprise can hamper the successful operation of
the latter. G. Abaimov, former chief of the production administration of Leningrad Sovnarkhoz, has stated that such
firms have received most of the plans instructing them as to
what to produce only in the first quarter of the year to which
the plans refer.   He emphasizes that such delay has placed
these factories in an extremely difficult position.

> There have been frequent instances in which the
> supplying and marketing organizations of the
> Sovnarkhoz R.S.F.S.R. have sent plants orders
> for delivery of metal and component products
> several months after the deadlines set for getting
> out the finished products.[45]

Responsibility for such great delays often lies with the
design institutes, but in many cases it is simply the result
of the extreme difficulty that the central planners encounter
when they seek to develop a coherent national plan which will
take into account the myriad of interrelationships existing

among the nation's economic activities. What complicates
the work of these firms even more is that individual chemical
enterprises either directly or through the supply organizations
often cancel previously issued orders for the manufacture of
specific equipment. At the Sumy Plant, the Kiev Bolshevik
Plant, and the Berdichev Progress Plant such refusals have
in some years averaged about 35 per cent of the total volume
of production. Sometimes the machinery and equipment which
has become no longer necessary can be altered to satisfy the
requirements of other customers. In many cases, however,
it accumulates in the warehouses of the firms and much
skilled labor of the firms' personnel has been expended without
achieving positive results. In addition to being wasteful in
itself, such a situation could be demoralizing to a conscientious
staff.

     Since the time of Adam Smith, economists have been aware
of the importance of specialization in production. A 1965
article by M. Mazo, a leading Soviet official in the area of
chemical machinery, provides a recent example of Soviet
thought on this subject.[46] He emphasizes that experience
had demonstrated the difficulty of introducing new technology
at unspecialized plants. In addition, the filling of countless
individual and small-series orders prevents the use of advanced mass-production equipment, continuous-flow production
methods, and modern technical-control procedures. Because
of this, the products of unspecialized plants are not only likely
to be of unnecessarily low quality but are also likely to be
unnecessarily expensive. In 1960 the All-Union Chemical
Machine Building Research and Design Institute developed a
plan upon which the specialization of chemical machine-
building firms could be based. This program was approved
by the central planning agencies. Nevertheless, those organizations in charge of distributing orders for the manufacture
of chemical equipment among the economic councils and
machine-building plants have systematically violated this plan.
A major cause of this neglect can be found in the fact that the
design institutes of the chemical industry, in their selection
of equipment for their blueprints, have not adhered to a
standardization of components. No powerful influence has
been capable of coordinating the efforts of all the institutions
and firms which deal with machinery and equipment in order
to achieve standardization and specialization. In the article
quoted above, Mazo states, "Thus the plan for the specialization
of chemical machine-building plants worked out in 1960 has
been frequently and grossly violated from the very outset."[47]

Successful operation of machine-building firms is also often hampered by lack of necessary raw materials or delay in their arrival at the plant. Earlier, mention was made of new types of steel, aluminum, and plastics which recently have become important in this area of the economy, and of the difficulties machinery enterprises have experienced in obtaining the quantities of these which their blueprints have demanded. Such difficulties also arise with regard to more commonly used raw materials. Here we enter the sphere of problems connected with the ordinary conduct of an economy where the production and allocation of all industrial inputs has been centrally planned. Decentralized flexibility is ruled out by the adoption of such an economic framework. Local enterprise directors cannot alter their production plans in conformity with the changing features of their environment. Information must be channeled through an organizational structure in which centralized decision making entails delay. The inability to forecast any particular production function precisely becomes a major impediment because such a function is itself an integral part of the production functions of other enterprises. When the Kommunarskiy Metallurgical Plant fails to produce the amount of two-ply steel which its planned quota had predicted, then the Urals Chemical Machine Building Plant, in its turn, must fail to produce some of the equipment on which certain chemical plants had counted, or at least the delivery of such equipment must be delayed until central planners can shift the appropriate steel from a project of lesser priority to the Urals Machine Building Plant.

It is apparent that many shortcomings have occurred within the walls of the machine-building factories themselves. Although they do not all fall neatly into distinct categories, many such shortcomings do share common features and can be found throughout Soviet industry. Storming is the name which has been applied to an obvious rush to fulfill the plan in the final days of the quarter. Following such a rush, a slack and disorganized period occurs in which the efforts of most plant personnel fall sharply until the next determined rush. Such a practice involves several problems for the customer. A piece of equipment which the supplier has promised to produce in a certain quarter and which it completes only in the final days will not reach the customer until well into the next quarter, perhaps several months after it was expected. Yet the machine builders are not penalized, for they have not broken the rules. As a result of storming, a large amount of equipment suddenly becomes available for transport to the

chemical plants, but this abrupt rush leads to a confusion
and delay in the delivery services. The chemical-fertilizer
enterprises suffer from a chronic shortage of spare parts.
This has led in many cases to the growth of elaborate repair
shops within the chemical firms, the purpose of which is to
construct those spare parts for the production of which the
plant cannot rely on the machine-building industry. The
Maardu Chemical Combine, for example, has experienced
great difficulties in obtaining certain spare parts for the
cranes which are used to scoop up superphosphate and transfer
it to machines which put it in bags for delivery. Such mechanisms are obviously essential for the plant to operate at full
capacity. The Tallin Machine Building Plant failed to comply
promptly with the Maardu requests for these spare parts
which it produces, even though the two firms are located in
the same city. [48]

The economic-planning framework currently employed by
the U.S.S.R. also enables individual machine-building plants
to cheat in regard to the promised quality of their output
without fear of risking the income of their employees or in-
curring major punishment from the government administration.
Many characteristics of the planning framework lead to such
cheating. The machine-building plant does not have to seek
its customers; the customers, on the other hand, cannot decide to cancel all future orders from those plants which they
believe produce shoddy equipment. In the past, it has been
the central administration at the sovnarkhoz and all-union
levels which has allocated the orders of chemical industries
to the manufacturers of machinery and equipment. Rarely
has a customer been free to return merchandise which it believed to be inferior, and even if the customer should do so
it has had no assurance that better-quality goods would be
sent to it later. In any case, such action would involve considerable delay which the customer could ill afford.

The machine-building firm gains no premium for fabri-
cating equipment of high quality. Restricted use of the price
mechanism in the past has not allowed price gradations based
upon many of the qualitative aspects of machinery. The producer and customer have not been able to bargain over price;
the customer has not even been able legally to go to an alternative supplier and voluntarily offer it a higher price for
equipment which he believes to be superior (although some
offers of this type are made and accepted illegally).
Innumerable instances arise, therefore, of production at
chemical-fertilizer plants being unsatisfactorily low because

of poor equipment. The supply of coke gas to the Gorlovka
Nitrogen Fertilizer Plant, located in the Ukraine, was interrupted for some months because the Sumy Machinery Plant
delivered compressors which had serious defects. The Volzhskiy Chemical Combine received apparatus from the Tambovk-
himmash Plant which was similarly useless. In this case,
the supplier refused for many months to heed requests for
machinery which would work.[49] In addition to such cases of
equipment which fails entirely to operate, we see many instances of breakdown within a matter of months or a few
years, necessitating repairs and spare parts; and, as we
have noted above, to obtain such spare parts is extremely
difficult.

Modern technical methods of quality control have been revised, so that a plant can ascertain the ability of its output
to withstand high pressures, extreme termperatures, and the
destructive action of acids. Special devices can even examine
products for defects such as cracks in the metal. Yet the
machine-building plants have been slow to put such devices
into practice. Their economic incentive to do so has appeared
certainly to be very small. In recent years it has become
imperative for each supplier to place its own special trade-
mark on all its products, so that it would be possible to determine the extent to which each firm is actually selling shoddy
equipment. Yet no organization has been established to undertake such a serious study in systematic detail. Without a
thorough study of all complaints by each firm's customers,
how can the central authorities determine whether a particular
firm should be punished as a result of a few complaints vehe-
ment enough to reach their ears, or whether that firm usually
sells machinery and equipment of satisfactory quality?
Occasional outbursts in the press seem the major form that
governmental criticism of poor quality has taken.

We have seen that organizations beyond the control of the
individual machine-building enterprise can and do hamper
the successful operation of the latter. Designers often are
late in constructing blueprints and the central planning organization adds to such delays. Cancellation of orders causes
confusion and often a waste of personnel efforts. Specialization has been thwarted and parts have not been standardized
to the extent considered desirable. Procedures for allocating
orders have been subjected to criticism. Lack of necessary
raw materials and delay in their arrival hinder the smooth
operation of the machine builders. Within the plant, storming,
reluctance to produce spare parts, and disregard of the quality

of its products all combine to create a situation which severely impedes the efforts of chemical firms to increase their output of chemical fertilizers and to improve the efficiency with which such fertilizers are produced.

PRODUCTION AND UTILIZATION
OF CHEMICAL FERTILIZERS

Several years ago a plant was built in Sverdlovsk for the manufacture of plastics, and was equipped with the most modern technology available at the time. After this new enterprise began operations, however, it discovered that it could find no buyers for the product of one of its shops. For two years this shop stood idle and then began to operate at only one-fifth of its designed capacity. Why should this happen? Around Moscow and in the Ukraine other plants were already supplying all the customers who had need for this product. In preparing their plans, individuals responsible for construction of this plant "did not study the demand which would be forthcoming, and did not correlate the volume of production and type of production with demand."[50]

A situation identical to this could not arise in the chemical fertilizer industry for some time, simply because the demand in the foreseeable future so greatly exceeds the supply. Yet the fertilizer industry does face numerous predicaments in the area of the marketing of its product. Even a "customer problem" exists. Although farms desire to obtain chemical fertilizers, the industrial enterprises do not know precisely where they should ship their merchandise until they are told by the government authorities. Delays in the relay of such information often occur. A 1964 article, for example, relates the case of the Karaganda Metallurgical Plant which succeeded in producing substantial above-plan quantities of ammonium sulphate. This extra output, however, was stranded in the plant's warehouse. Government officials responsible for allocating the fertilizer were unable to decide upon a consignee for shipment.[51] The Kalinin Plant which produces enriched insecticides and herbicides accumulated large quantities of these in its warehouses at one point in 1963. Two shops were in danger of stoppage because of lack of further storage facilities, yet the plant could not prod government organizations into providing information concerning deliveries. When confronted with this development by a

correspondent of Trud, the chief of Soyuzglavkhim replied
that according to his data this particular plant was not to have
begun operations for some time. The fact that the plant had
been completed ahead of schedule had not yet filtered up
through the government bureaucracy, and hence no orders had
been issued as to allocation of its output. [52] The Riga Polyethylene Products Plant in Latvia makes irrigation hose of
black polyethylene as well as polyvinyl film which can replace
glass in hotbeds or greenhouses as a protection for early
plants and can also be used to line silo pits. Both of these
products have become important for agriculture. Yet an
official at the plant claims that often at the beginning of a
month they do not know where to ship the products or in what
quantities. This can cause confusion and a slowdown of
operations at the plant.

Poor coordination of information regarding deliveries is
not the only source of marketing problems for chemical industries providing products to be used in agriculture. Liquid
ammonia presents an interesting example of a more basic
coordination problem. In 1962 the Shechekino and Novomoskovsk Combines in Tul'skaya oblast experienced great difficulty in marketing nitrogenous fertilizers of this kind. Liquid
ammonia not only is an effective fertilizer but also is said to
possess the advantage that it is much simpler and less expensive to produce than are solid forms such as ammonium
nitrate. What has hindered its sale? Special facilities are
necessary for this product. Ordinary railroad cars are not
satisfactory. Special tank cars and tank trucks must be built
to deliver liquid ammonia. Special machines have to be de-
vised for applying this fertilizer to the soil. Depots have to
be constructed at railway terminals to store the liquid until
farms send tank trucks to pick it up. Small amounts of the
necessary equipment have begun to aid in solving this problem.
The Kapsukas Automatic Food Machinery Plant in Lithuania
has organized the production of special GAN-8 machines for
applying these fertilizers to the soil. Yet, in general,
authorities have not tackled the problem, and some have even
urged that production of liquid fertilizers be cut back rather
than that the necessary facilities be increased. The result
has been confusion at certain fertilizer plants and a waste of
production facilities. Some areas of the country, such as the
Irkutsk oblast, have solved the problem on the basis of local
initiative, particularly by firm authorities who have managed
to improvise in construction of necessary facilities.

A similar predicament has arisen in the delivery of liquid herbicides which seem more effective and easier to apply than powder forms. With sulphuric acid, which is used in the manufacture of superphosphate fertilizers, the delivery problem has also appeared since some sulphuric acid is produced from wastes at copper smelting plants and then must be transported to the relevant fertilizer enterprises. In 1964 Kosygin noted that the pipeline transport of oil and gas was growing very rapidly, and he predicted that deliveries by this form of transportation would be increased by almost 35 per cent within a year. [53] This policy of removing from the railroads the burden of shipping oil and oil products will no doubt leave more room for the transport of products discussed above, particularly since the tank cars previously used for oil can be converted to the delivery of liquid ammonia and herbicides. It remains a fact, however, that basic coordination between output of the latter and production of the special equipment necessary for their delivery and application has entailed considerable delay.

We have referred above to the Karaganda Metallurgical Plant and the fact that its warehouses contained excess amounts of ammonium sulphate because the government officials responsible for allocating orders for delivery had failed in their duty. At this point we should note that the ammonium sulphate which was stored soon absorbed moisture, caked, and became a solid mass. It then could not be removed without the aid of miners' picks. The chemical fertilizer industry has faced serious difficulties in regard to such caking of its products. Khrushchev in many speeches referred to the huge piles of fertilizers standing by the railway siding while the farms to which they had been assigned did not bother to claim them. Deterioration of fertilizers into a useless mass explains this phenomenon. Such deterioration can be avoided by improved production techniques which result in granulation of the fertilizer and by packaging of fertilizers in moisture-proof bags. [54] In the production and sale of nonliquid chemical fertilizers a most important bottleneck has been the inability of fertilizer enterprises to acquire a sufficient number of paper bags in which to pack their product. In a letter written on June 24, 1963, to the Supreme Council of the National Economy, Kadyshev, the Chairman of the Central Asian Sovnarkhoz, stated that a lack of paper bags had created an extremely difficult situation for many chemical plants with regard to their fulfilling the plan for the production and delivery of fertilizer to agriculture. Such enterprises required

40 million paper bags for 1963, but only 28.3 million were allocated to them. A prior request by Kadyshev, presumably to a lower authority than the Supreme Council, was denied. [55]

What can present a problem here is not just the shortage of ordinary paper bags. Because of the danger of caking which we have discussed above, the bags used to pack chemical fertilizers should be of a special type. Realizing this, a government authority developed a "State Standard" bag, having five thicknesses of bituminized paper, which all fertilizer enterprises were to use. Unfortunately, production of such a bag lagged seriously behind the demand for it. For example, the Lisichansk Chemical Combine, located in the Ukraine, found that it repeatedly lacked the necessary number of standard bags. Even though the ammonium nitrate which it produces is granulated, nevertheless, such a fertilizer spoils quickly in ordinary paper bags. About one-third of the Lisichansk output, at least until 1964, was shipped in inferior bags. [56] The Dneprodzerzhinsk Nitrogen Fertilizer Plant for many months after it commenced production still did not have the equipment necessary for closing its fertilizer containers.

In order to increase the output of chemical fertilizers, the Soviet leadership has had to take into account continually the existence of interindustry economic relations. Successful mobilization of the fertilizer industry has required the simultaneous expansion of numerous other industries and, in cases where the latter have failed to expand, the fertilizer industry has been severely hampered. Paper bags seem indeed a very small item. Yet lack of enough bags and the supplying of the wrong type of bags have been able to ruin huge amounts of fertilizer, restrict the effectiveness of much more, and slow down production at the fertilizer enterprises. In July, 1964, P. Kazakov in an article concerning the "Lagging Production of Fertilizer Containers" claimed that no improvement had yet been made in this situation. [57] When discussing the new facilities made necessary by the manufacture of liquid fertilizers, we mentioned the transportation difficulties which such fertilizers encountered because of their peculiar nature. We should note, however, that serious shortages of railroad capacity have been experienced by plants making even nonliquid fertilizers. The Lisichansk Chemical Combine, mentioned earlier, has had to slow down its operations frequently because of such shortages, after hundreds of tons of ammonium nitrate and carbamide had accumulated in its warehouses. The Riga Superphosphate Plant and the Karaganda Metallurgical Plant have also, for example, endured deficiencies in their rail transport. Delays in the delivery of fertilizers become particularly important when the fertilizers are being kept in bags of inferior quality where moisture can render them useless.

V. Kosov has mentioned that, in order to raise the interest of chemical enterprises in improving quality, fertilizer plants have been given permission to raise prices on the sale of out- puts containing higher amounts of plant nutrients than those required by the state standards. He notes, however, that such a practice has led to confusion. The government administration previously has determined how many tons of each fertilizer (nutrients plus ballast) should be sent to each farm. Then if the fertilizer plant produces the proper amount of nutrients but delivers them in a more concentrated form than expected, the government calculations will no longer be appropriate. Some farms will get the proper total weight (but an extra supply of nutrients) while other farms may receive nothing. The fact that Kosov is very disturbed by this possibility wit- nesses to the lack of flexibility which central planning neces- sarily causes, even in regard to a simple recalculation of numbers.[58]

When discussing the problems involved in the marketing of liquid ammonia, we noted that many kolkhoz and sovkhoz are poorly prepared to receive and utilize liquid fertilizers. In a great number of cases such a situation also exists with regard to ordinary chemical fertilizers. A major shortage has arisen in the number of machines for applying the new granulated types of fertilizers made necessary, as we have seen, by the danger of caking. Most fertilizer still is not of the mixed or compound variety, yet the majority of farms lack equipment for local mining of chemical fertilizers. Serious criticism has also sprung up concerning the quality of the equipment that has been provided for the above duties.

"Now when the scale of production and application of fertilizer in our country is growing rapidly, it is extremely important to avoid mistakes in its utilization." With these words, Professors I. Gunar and P. Naidin raise an issue of great concern. The U.S.S.R. possesses a wide variety of soils. "This demands the accurate determination of those regions where chemical fertilizers should be applied first and the most effective procedures for applying them."[59] Not all soils lack the same plant nutrients and to apply those types of which a given field already has a sufficient amount would be largely to waste such surplus nutrients. Hence an extensive system for analyzing soils and for recommending

the proper types to be used is mandatory for efficient allocation. An important aspect of this problem is the lack of
specialists trained in agricultural chemistry. In an article
which emphasizes this shortage, four Soviet scientists have
noted that there are only two agricultural chemistry faculties
in the entire Russian Republic and their enrollment is only
100 persons.

> . . . the majority of the specialists who have
> finished higher educational institutions or tech-
> nicums are very poorly prepared in agricultural
> chemistry and are unable to solve many practical
> problems in a qualified manner. Fertilizers are
> frequently applied where they are not needed the
> most, without a preliminary chemical analysis of
> the soil and not in the doses and combinations that
> are most effective under the specific conditions . . .
> It is indisputable that there are insufficient agricul-
> tural chemistry laboratories in the villages, and
> many of the existing ones are not staffed by experi-
> enced cadres. [60]

The authors conclude that merely by using the existing levels
of fertilizer production more rationally it would be possible
to increase their effectiveness by at least 25 to 30 per cent.

In March, 1964, a Plenary Session of the CPSU Central
Committee formally declared that it considered necessary
"the creation of a single agrochemical service in the country
for the purpose of utilizing more correctly the supply of
mineral fertilizers and other chemical agents available for
agriculture."[61] It emphasized the necessity of establishing
agrochemical laboratories furnished with modern equipment
to perform mass analyses of soils, fertilizers and fodders,
and thereby to render concrete aid to the collective and state
farms in the chemicalization of farming and animal husbandry.
It also urged the Central Committees of the Union-Republic
Party Committees and other responsible officials to create a
network of schools, courses, and seminars both formally
within the educational system and informally within the collective and state farms for the purpose of training a large
group of agrochemical workers capable of organizing the
effective utilization of chemical fertilizers, herbicides, and
insecticides, and the mechanization of their application. With
the reforms that increase local responsibility for decisions
concerning agricultural production, this need for adequately
trained specialists will clearly be intensified.

PLANNING AND ADMINISTRATIVE REFORMS

The party and government administration in the U.S.S.R. is not satisfied with the present effectiveness of chemical fertilizers. Two broad types of reform are now being implemented in an attempt to raise this effectiveness. In the past, the government has established certain quality standards for each type of fertilizer product, and factories are supposed to adhere to these regulations. One obvious reform is to raise such standards. As will be noted, however, criticism has been levied against the inflexibility of this system. The government has been slow in changing required standards as technology has improved. In addition, violations of the regulations concerning quality seem to be frequent. Increasing attention is being paid to the need to use chemical fertilizer in such a way as to yield the greatest benefit. Scientific examinations of the structure and requirements of soil are now being undertaken throughout the U.S.S.R., so that each type of soil will receive that type of fertilizer which is best suited for it. Changes such as these represent an attempt to improve central planning and central administration. The other broad type of reform is quite different. Individual enterprises are being granted greater autonomy in production and investment decisions, in the hope that local decision making in this sphere will be better able than central planning to take into consideration all the production problems of the firm and to weigh rationally all the alternative investment possibilities.

The first type of economic reform mentioned above differs in a most important manner from the second reform. It relies entirely on central planning and on centralized decision making. Indeed, the fertilizer allocation as envisaged above calls for a substantial expansion of the responsibility of central planners, with reliance upon electronic computers and modern methods of data analysis. The second reform, on the other hand, reflects a dissatisfaction with centralized decision making. It entails a greater emphasis upon cost calculations in terms of rubles within each industrial enterprise, and it provides for the use of such decentralized calculations as a basis for production and investment decisions. Given a set of prices for final products and a required output mix, it is hoped that this emphasis upon monetary cost per unit of output will result in cost-reducing innovations or alterations of inputs. Profit is seen as an index of success in this endeavor and as a useful base for determination of bonuses.

Quality Standards

An inspector whose occupation is to supervise adherence
to government standards in the fertilizer industry wrote in
1965, "The fact is that almost all state standards dealing
with mineral fertilizer are outdated."[62] The 1965 regulations
concerning ammonium nitrate were introduced in 1958, concerning phosphorous in 1952, concerning potassium chloride
in 1950, and concerning granulated superphosphate in 1953.
This inspector envisaged a more rapid revision of required
standards in order to force factories to improve the quality
of their products whenever new processes and equipment become available to them. He emphasized at the same time,
however, that even current regulations were violated frequently.

> With selective examination of the production of the
> Sumgait Combine, it was discovered that more than
> 30 per cent of the superphosphate does not corres-
> pond to the required standards concerning granu-
> lated structure.[63]

Deterioration of the product during transportation and storage
becomes inevitable. The problem of proper containers for
chemical fertilizer has already been mentioned. Shestakov,
the inspector quoted above, noted that this problem is made
worse because factories pour fertilizers into the containers
while the former are still hot, thus causing the bags to break.
Yet there are no standards "to require them to cool the chemical product to a definite temperature before packaging."[64]
Potassium fertilizers are not processed in such a way as to
prevent their caking. Phosphorous and superphosphate fertilizers contain too much moisture. The central argument of
Shestakov's article is that "many standards do not stimulate
the struggle of enterprises towards high quality production."[65]
Evidence even in this article, however, suggests that the
Stalin-Khrushchev system of central planning fails to improve
the quality of products not merely because standards are outdated, but rather because officials at the level of the industrial
firm do not find it in the firm's interest or in their own interest
to improve quality. If the latter position is accurate, then revisions of quality standards are not likely of themselves to
lead to significant improvements. In addition, we might well
note that, to be most effective, special standards would have
to be determined separately for each product of each factory.
The reason for this necessity is that the types of machinery
and equipment being produced for this industry are changing
rapidly; some are even being imported. No two factories
possess the same plant and equipment, and so no two factories
possess the same capabilities.

Soil Studies

"As shown by numerous experiments over many years, without the introduction of lime the positive action of acid fertilizers is extinguished . . . and sometimes turns into a negative action; that is, in sections where mineral fertilizer was applied the yield proved to be even lower than in sections without fertilizer."[66] This can happen in areas where the soil possesses high acidity and the particular fertilizer applied tends to increase this acidity.[67] Soils differ widely in regard to those particular nutrients that they lack. Crops also differ in regard to the relative amounts of nutrients that they require. Each nutrient can be applied in different forms. As noted in the above quotation, it is even possible that application of a certain type of fertilizer to a certain soil may actually reduce crop yields. Allocation and utilization of chemical fertilizers is, therefore, of vital importance in determining their impact on agricultural production. The words of P. Kravshenko emphasize this point:

> How should the funds of chemical fertilizers be apportioned in order to receive the maximum possible gross increase in agricultural production? With the existing system of planning in this business, errors and miscalculations are inevitable. Why? The reason is this, that the planning organization does not have available information concerning the effectiveness of fertilizers, applied under different crops with regard to their quality structure, their soil differences, etc. . . . the element of chance in such a distribution plays an appreciable role.[68]

And Z. Nuriev says:

> The interests of a more efficient chemicalization of agriculture urgently require us to raise agrochemical service significantly, to strengthen the essential agrochemical laboratories, to expand their networks and to speed up work on the study of the agrochemical characteristics of the soil.[69]

An increase in information is urgently required. What should be done with this additional information? How should it be utilized to achieve a more effective allocation of chemical fertilizers? A common answer is that the central-planning administration should receive and consider the additional information, and that it should coordinate allocation plans to maximize their effectiveness. P. Kravshenko has expressed confidence in the ability of electronic computers to aid central

planners in this sphere. He notes that in the All-Union
Scientific Research Institute of Agricultural Economics
(VNIECX), at which he is an instructor, "special methods
and economic-mathematical models have been created" for
this purpose.

Thus the development of electronic computers has created
hopes for the preservation and improvement of the framework
of central planning. Whether such hopes will be fulfilled--
whether the channels of communication between each farm
and the planning administration will permit a flow of information which is accurate and can be revised readily, whether
computers can digest all relevant information, compare the
benefits that can be obtained from the allocation of different
combinations of nutrients to each farm, and provide allocation
recommendations--all this remains to be seen.[70] It is
possible that a movement in this direction can improve the
present effectiveness of chemical fertilizer. The key question
is how the results of such a development might compare with
the results of a shift to decentralized decision making.

Decentralized Decision Making

In the first quarter of 1966, forty-three enterprises in
various branches of industry were transferred to a new type
of planning framework. Among these were, for example, the
Urals factory of heavy-machine building which produces some
of the equipment used in chemical fertilizer plants and the
Voskresensk Chemical Combine which produces fertilizers.[71]
Other firms have been transferred to this framework rather
systematically. There is, in the recent planning changes, a
new "emphasis on lowering costs in ruble terms" and "on
strengthening the factory's financial independence from the
state . . . Thus the new system of planning and economic
stimulation demands a radical improvement in the system
of accounting, operational and statistical calculation, and
primarily in the calculation of costs with the estimation of
expenditures on production."[72] An article in the Ekonomicheskaya gazeta has examined in detail the recent administrative changes in the Voskresensk Chemical Combine.

From now on substantial independence has been
given to the enterprises. In particular, they have
received the right, owing to the decentralization
of capital investment, to change equipment in accordance with their own discoveries, to institute
new technology, and to put into effect other arrange-
ments for increasing the efficiency of production.

    Now the organization and structure of administra-
tion are also their internal affair. [73]

According to the new system, each enterprise accumulates an
investment fund. To this fund are added "part of the profits,
30 per cent of the depreciation deductions, and the receipts
from the liquidation of unnecessary equipment."

    In this reform, we see a major alteration of previous
administrative practices. The nature of this alteration con-
trasts sharply with the reforms of quality standards and soil
studies discussed above, in that here detailed central planning
and centralized administration are being discarded as inappropriate for the tasks facing modern Soviet industry. It
is hoped that the new system will improve both the investment
process on the one hand and also day-to-day factory operation
on the other. B. Vasilev, chief engineer of the Voskresensk
Chemical Combine, has emphasized that "until now in our
plan for new technology higher authorities could retain one
[program] and strike out another, although who knows better
than the workers in the factory, themselves, which of the
possible programs are necessary?" There is a widespread
feeling that the higher authorities, particularly in the recent
years of industrial diversification and expansion, have not
been able to maintain a comprehensive knowledge of each
individual factory and that, because of this, investment programs could be better formulated by the officials within each
factory. The calculation of ruble costs now has acquired new
significance. Lowering ruble costs will increase a factory's
profits and hence its investment or development fund. Calculation of costs can provide a guide to the weighing of alternative investment programs, and hence has become essential
for the decentralization of investment decisions. Greater
emphasis upon the calculation of ruble costs also may affect
the day-to-day operations of the factory. As the Voskresensk
chief engineer has said, "Now, for example, we take better
care of the utilization of valuable waste materials." [74]

    An additional aspect of the decentralization reforms de-
serves comment at this point: although general government
policy in regard to these reforms was decreed in 1964, the
pace of actual implementation has been slow. It appears that,
in spite of a conscientious desire on the part of political
leaders, several years have been necessary in order to shift
from the first framework of detailed central planning towards
the second framework of decentralized decision making and
responsibility. Writing in 1968, for example, the U.S.S.R.
Minister of Nonferrous Metallurgy claimed that:

The reform has not yet touched our research and
design organizations.   They have little stake in the
high quality of designs and bear almost no material
responsibility for miscalculations.

The solution lies in the introduction of economic
accountability into the entire chain of collectives on
the path to new technology, from science to production: at the research and design institutes, at construction sites and at enterprises.   Then, at what-
ever stage a delay may occur, the guilty party will
feel the consequences thereof, including material
consequences, and the possibility of mistakes and
miscalculations will be reduced to a minimum. [75]

Definite steps have been taken towards decentralization,
and such steps have received favorable comments in the Soviet
press; yet this movement towards a new planning framework
has seemed to be slow.   Some research and university institutions have signed contracts with enterprises in regard to
solving specific problems that the latter face, yet the use of
such direct ties could be expanded much further. [76]   R. Ismailov,
President of the Azerbaidzhan Republic Academy of Sciences,
stated in 1968 that the experimental-production facilities of
the research institutions were still deficient to a major degree
and that coordination should perhaps be achieved by uniting
scientific establishments, design institutes and industrial
firms into a number of integrated organizations to accelerate
technological progress. [77]

It has been possible to interpret the slow pace of the decentralization reforms as an indication of failure; it has been
possible, at any date since 1964, to conclude that the planning
framework existing at that particular moment was not and
could not be a success.   Some Western writers have viewed
the reforms in this manner; and this interpretation has led
them to an attitude of pessimism and a belief that the reforms
are doomed.   On the other hand, it is possible to regard the
decentralization reforms as a broad and long-run movement,
and to see any particular set of regulations as simply one
resting place in an exploration in which the U.S.S.R. is continually seeking improvements in its planning framework.
From this view, one can consider many practices in post-1964
planning as experimental in nature; and one can understand
the slow pace of reform implementation and even reversals
of certain government policies, as a rational method of experimentation.   In my opinion, the latter view is appropriate,
and so much of the following discussion of the decentralization

reforms is based upon the interpretation of the reforms as a long-run movement in which various policies are being adopted as experimental attempts to understand the advantages and shortcomings of the new planning framework

NOTES

1.   V. C. Lelchuk, The Creation of the Chemical Industry of the U.S.S.R. (Moscow: published by Nauka, 1964), p. 146.

2.   Ibid., p. 111.

3.   Ibid., p. 206.

4.   Ibid., p. 175.

5.   S. I. Bolfkobich, L. I. Dubovitsky, and N. A. Simulin, "The Production of Mineral Fertilizers" in The Chemical Industry of the U.S.S.R. (Moscow: The State Scientific-Technical Publishers of Chemical Literature, 1959), p. 261.

6.   Articles discussing these three shortcomings in detail can be found in Ekonomicheskaya gazeta, 51 (1964) and 4, 10, 13, 27 (1965). Other references are mentioned later.

7.   Directives of the Twenty-third Congress on the 1966-1970 plan, Ekonomicheskaya gazeta, 8 (1966), 6-7.

8.   A. N. Kosygin, "Speech to the Twenty-third Congress of the CPSU, Ekonomicheskaya gazeta, 14 (1966) 8.

9.   N. S. Khrushchev, "Development of the Chemical Industry," Plenary Session of the Central Committee CPSU, Pravda (May 10, 1958), pp. 1-4; as translated in The Current Digest of the Soviet Press (June 18, 1958), p. 12.

10.   Ibid.

11.   Ibid.

12.   Ibid.

13.   V. Gutyrya, Vice-President of the Academy of
Sciences UkSSR (Ukranian Soviet Socialist Republic), Pravda
Ukrainy (November 28, 1963), p. 2.

14.   Ibid., p. 2.

15.   For a general criticism of the relationship between
scientific research and industrial application of the results of
research, see Pravda (May 4, 1963), p. 2. This article,
"Pay Special Attention to the Development of Chemistry, "
presents a discussion held by the Moscow City Party Committee on this subject.

16.   See, for example, an article by V. Koval, Deputy
Minister of the Chemical Industry of the U.S.S.R., "The
Chemical Industry--Its Importance for Agriculture, "
Ekonomicheskaya gazeta 46 (1965), 19-20.

17.   M. Koton, "Obstacles to the Introduction of the
Attainments of Chemical Science into Industry, " Ekonomicheskaya gazeta, 45 (November 9, 1963), 6.

18.   N. S. Khrushchev, "The Development of the Chemical Industry, " Pravda (May 10, 1958), pp. 1-4.

19.   N. S. Khrushchev, "Speech at the Plenary Session
of the Central Committee of CPSU, " Pravda (February 15,
1964), p. 6.

20.   Aliyeva, "Why New Petrochemical Processes Are
Applied Slowly, " Izvestiya (June 8, 1965), p. 3.

21.   Ibid.

22.   Ibid.

23.   See, in this regard, Professors N. Yermolenko and
M. Pavlyuchenko, "Byelorussia Needs Mineral Fertilizers, "
Izvestiya (May 21, 1958), 3; and V. Martynovskiy, "The Importance of Mineral Fertilizers to Agriculture, " Ekonomicheskaya gazeta 45 (1963), 30.

24.   For an account of this development see V. Koptelov
et al., "Higher Labor Productivity at the Kemerovo Nitrogen
Fertilizer Plant, " Trud (September 28, 1963), p. 1.

25.   B. Prudnikova, Sovetskaya Moldaviya (October 12, 1963), p. 3; translated in JPRS: 22, 455; OTS: 64-21121; U.S.S.R. Industrial Development, 130, 8-10.

26.   Ye. Sadovskiy, Sovetskaya Byelorussia (October 18, 1963), p. 21; translated in JPRS: 22, 671; OTS: 64-21248; U.S.S.R. Industrial Development, 133 (January 9, 1964), 15.

27.   L. Kulikovsky, "Unproductive Institutes," Izvestiya (May 28, 1964), p. 3.

28.   M. Kolobkov, V. Boyko and S. Laptev, "Produce More Fertilizers for West Siberia," Pravda (October 9, 1963), p. 2.

29.   Yu. Sergeyev and O. Tereshchenko, "New Technology and Patents," Kommunist 8 (May, 1965), 65-72.

30.   B. Vasilyev, Candidate of Technical Sciences, "Making Use of Discoveries," Izvestiya (July 29, 1964), p. 3.

31.   B. Dubovnikov, Vice-Chairman of the Volga Economic Council, "A Machine Begins with the Design," Pravda (September 4, 1964), p. 2.

32.   A. Kuramzhin, "The Planning and Production of Chemical Machines," Pravda (November 18, 1963), p. 2.

33.   V. Krotov, Izvestiya (October 20, 1963), p. 2.

34.   For an account of this, see Trud (November 26, 1963), p. 2.

35.   For general discussions of this subject, with criticisms of the present network of design institutes, see V. Bushuyev, director of the CPSU Central Committee's Chemical Industry Department, "The Economy Demands the Development of Chemistry," Pravda (August 3, 1965), p. 2; B. Dubovnikov, Vice-Chairman of the Volga Economic Council, "A Machine Begins with the Design," Pravda (September 4, 1964), p. 2; and "Pay Special Attention to the Development of Chemistry," a discussion within the Moscow City Party Committee, Pravda (May 4, 1963), p. 2.

36.   V. Sofronov, "Design Errors at the Sredneuralsk Copper Smelting Plant," Ekonomicheskaya gazeta 33 (August 17, 1963), 11.

37.   Ekonomicheskaya gazeta 43 (October 26, 1963), 14.

38.   L. Glikman, "Problems in Supplying the Chemical Industry with Machinery and Equipment," Ekonomicheskaya gazeta 45 (November 9, 1963), 11.

39.   V. Burenkov, Kazakhstanskaya Pravda (October 8, 1963), pp. 1-3.

40.   V. Parfenov, "Accelerating the Utilization of New Capacity," Pravda (October 14, 1963), p. 2.

41.   Ibid.

42.   D. Orechkin, Candidate of Technical Sciences, "The Firms Await Scientists," Izvestiya, (August 20, 1964), p. 3.

43.   Ibid.

44.   A. Kosygin, "Speech to the Supreme Soviet," Pravda (December 10, 1964), p. 1.

45.   G. Abaimov, Ekonomicheskaya gazeta 46 (1963), 5.

46.   M. Mazo, "Machines for Chemistry," Pravda (February 21, 1965), p. 2.

47.   Ibid.

48.   "The Maardu Chemical Combine," JPRS: 22, 805; OTS: 64-21337; The Soviet Chemical Industry, 139 (January 20, 1964), 1-2.

49.   K. Voinov, "Status of Construction at the Volzhskiy Chemical Combine," Trud (November 29, 1963), p. 1.

50.   Ekonomicheskaya gazeta (December 7, 1963), pp. 9-10.

51.   Komsomolskaya Pravda (January 11, 1964), p. 1.

52.   Loginov, Zotov, Manakin and Kolesnikov, "Overproduction of Herbicides, " Trud (October 23, 1963), p. 1.

53.   A. Kosyзin, Pravda (December 10, 1964), p. 1.

54.   For a detailed discussion of the scientific techniques
involved in the granulation process, see Robert Noyes, Potash
and Potassium Fertilizers (Noyes Development Corporation,
1966), pp. 102 and 149-151. Also see C. J. Pratt and Robert
Noyes, Nitrogen Fertilizer Chemical Processes (Noyes Development Corporation, 1965), pp. 22-33, 53, and 86-89.

55.   Kadyshev, Ekonomicheskaya gazeta (August 31, 1963),
p. 17.

56.   Even at the end of 1965, the director of the Lisichansk
Chemical Combine claimed that this problem was still of
major importance. See in this regard the article by V. Gogin,
Ekonomicheskaya gazeta, 46, (1965), 21.

57.   P. Kazakov, "Lagging Production of Fertilizer Containers, " Ekonomicheskaya gazeta (July 25, 1964), p. 3.

58.   V. Kosov, Pravda (February 9, 1965), p. 2.

59.   I. Gunar and P. Naidin, Pravda (February 24, 1965),
pp. 2-3.

60.   V. Klechkovsky, member of the V. I. Lenin All-
Union Academy of Agricultural Sciences, and Candidates of
Agricultural Sciences P. Smirnov, B. Bagayev, and B.
Pushkov, "Rural Areas Await Experienced Agricultural
Chemists, " Pravda (September 12, 1963), p. 2.

61.   Central Committee CPSU, Pravda (February 16,
1964), p. 1.

62.   A. Shestakov, "The Quality of Vitamins of the
Fields, " Ekonomicheskaya gazeta (May 12, 1965), p. 14.

63.   Ibid.

64.   Ibid.

65.   Ibid.

66.   V. Pannikov, "Chemical Land Improvement--a Dependable Means of Attaining High Yields," Ekonomicheskaya
gazeta, 18 (May, 1966), 7.

67.   We should note that a major program for the treatment
of acid soils with lime has been developed in the past two years
(1965-1966).   Several recent articles discuss this program.
See, for example, "Chemical Land Improvement," Ekonomicheskaya gazeta, 24 (1966), 36-37.   This program should
increase the effectiveness of chemical fertilizer in large areas
of the nation.

68.   P. Kravshenko, "Fertilizers--their Precise Allocation," Ekonomicheskaya gazeta, 18 (1966), 29.

69.   Z. Nuriev, "The Grain Economy of Bashkira,"
Ekonomicheskaya gazeta, 9 (March, 1966), 14-15.

70.   Kravshenko has estimated that "for the most modest
calculation it would be necessary to compare more than four
million plots."

71.   See Ekonomicheskaya gazeta, 5 (February, 1966), 4-5.

72.   Ibid.

73.   Iakovshuk, Ekonomicheskaya gazeta, 6 (February,
1966), 13.

74.   Ibid.

75.   P. Lomako, U.S.S.R. Minister of Nonferrous
Metallurgy, "The Reform and Technological Progress in the
Branches," Pravda (May 21, 1968), 2-3; as translated in the
Current Digest of the Soviet Press, XX, 21, 22-23.

76.   See, for example, V. Karmazin, "Contracts with
Enterprises," Pravda (May 23, 1968), p. 2.

77.   R. Ismailov, "The Yield of Scientific Research,"
Pravda (July 3, 1968), p. 3.

CHAPTER 3   IRRIGATION AND DRAINAGE

INVESTMENT PLANS

> I have already emphasized that we are concentrating
> on increasing the production of chemical fertilizers
> and applying them in the most efficient way, while
> irrigation comes second. This is not because we
> under-estimate the importance of irrigation, but be-
> cause we are not in a position to solve these two tasks
> at the same time. [1]

As can be seen from the above quotation, as late as
October, 1963, the official position of the Soviet government
was that restraint should be placed upon investments in
irrigation and drainage. "Irrigation construction requires
huge capital expenditures and a good deal of time . . ."[2]
Land reclamation was considered to be a worthwhile goal,
and even a necessary goal, but the government was not yet
prepared to use those funds, set aside for the intensification
of agriculture, to develop this particular sector. Rather,
the Soviet position was to emphasize production of farm
machinery and the expansion and improvement of facilities
producing chemical fertilizers. As noted in Chapter 1, a
resolution of the Plenary Session of the CPSU on February
15, 1964, described a program of irrigation and drainage as
one of the three paths along which the intensification of agricultural production should proceed. It recommended "expanding and improving research in the field of irrigation and
agricultural water supply, as well as hydraulic construction
and land drainage. Special attention must be given to the
working out of highly productive methods of watering, rational
irrigation systems, and effective drainage."[3] In September,
1963, K. K. Shubladze, Director of the U.S.S.R. Ministry
of Agriculture's Water Resources Administration, stated:
"Almost 9 million hectares are under irrigation at the present
time. In order to fulfill successfully the task, that has been

set by our party, of sharply increasing agricultural production, we must increase the area of irrigated land to 28 million hectares by 1980.[4] Shubladze emphasized the enormity of this prospective program by noting that "in the last ten years the area of irrigated land has increased by only 1.2 million hectares."[5]

When Khrushchev retired, the U.S.S.R. did have experience in the area of irrigation and drainage; it planned in the near future to implement a large-scale expansion of this sector, but it had not adopted a definite time schedule. Within six months of Khrushchev's retirement, Brezhnev stated in a speech to the Plenary Session of the CPSU Central Committee:

> I should like to lay special stress on the importance of the further development of irrigation in arid regions and of land reclamation in zones of excessive moisture. In the next five years it is planned to carry out work on irrigating an area of more than three million hectares and draining six million hectares. This will be a great deal of work. . . These must be real engineering projects, carried out on the level of modern water-resources construction. . . Measures for combatting soil erosion are also envisaged in the national-economic plan, and the necessary financial and material resources will be allocated for these purposes.[6]

In February, 1966, the directives of the Twenty-third Congress of the Communist Party resolved, during the new five-year plan (1966-1970), to implement a broad program of land improvements:

> . . . in the non-black-earth zone of the Russian Federation, the Belorussian Republic, the Baltic Republics and the western provinces and wooded regions of the Ukraine, as well as in the Far East, to drain an area of 6 million to 6.5 million hectares of swampy and overly moist land, to carry out the technical improvement of about 9 million hectares and the liming of not less than 28 million hectares of acid soils.

> . . . to organize work on the irrigation of 2.5-3 million hectares of land in arid regions. In addition to enlarging the area of irrigated lands in the republics of Central Asia and the Transcaucasus, there must be broad development of irrigation in the Northern Caucasus, along the Volga, in the southern part of the Ukraine, and in the Kazakh and Moldavian Republics.[7]

In May, 1966, Brezhnev underlined the seriousness of
this program. "A highly important matter now, in our opinion,
is land reclamation in the broad sense in which we have been
discussing this question at the Plenary Session of the Party
Central Committee. We must realize and say firmly to the
entire Party, the entire people that this is not a transitory
campaign, that it is a program in the sphere of agriculture
calculated for a long period, a program requiring immense
efforts and large capital investments and material and technical resources."[8] Brezhnev noted that in the twenty years from
1946 until 1965 the state invested only 5.6 billion rubles in
the construction of water-resources systems, while the Five
Year Plan for the years 1966 through 1970 provided for an investment of more than 10 billion rubles for this purpose.
Ye. Ye. Alekseveysky, U.S.S.R. Minister of Land Reclamation and Water Resources, has estimated that for the period
1966-1970, when all sources of financing are considered,
more than 15 billion rubles will have been spent on various
land reclamation measures.[9] Nor is this program to diminish
in scope after 1970. A resolution of the Plenary Session of
the CPSU Central Committee in May, 1966, forsees "an
expansion in the area of irrigated land by seven million to
eight million hectares and of drained land by fifteen million
to sixteen million hectares in the next ten years; the total of
reclaimed land in the country to reach between thirty-seven
million and thirty-nine million hectares in 1975."[10] In March,
1965 Brezhnev stated that, "Beginning this year, the state
will assume the cost of work on liming and land reclamation."[11]
In April, 1965, a resolution of the CPSU Central and the
U.S.S.R. Council of Ministers elaborated the government's
policy in this regard.

> The CPSU Central Committee and the U.S.S.R.
> Council of Ministers, attaching great importance to
> the carrying out of land reclamation, the liming of
> acid soils, and the implementation of other measures
> aimed at raising the fertility of the land, have estab-
> lished that work on the fundamental improvement of
> collective farm lands (the construction and recon-
> struction of closed drainage and open intra-farm
> drainage networks, the clearing of trees and brush
> and other engineering work; the complex of opera-
> tions involved in cutting, transporting, and using
> peat; the liming of acid soils, including the cost of
> lime fertilizers and schistous ash and expenditures
> on shipping them and spreading them on the soil)

and work on the gypsuming of strongly alkaline soils
on the collective farms, including the cost of the
gypsum and expenditures on shipping it and spreading
it on the soil, as well as the expenditures for com-
piling design-and-decumentation for the above-mentioned work, will be carried out through state budget
funds allocated for operating expenditures in conformity with the volume of work envisaged in the national-
economic plans. Work on the fundamental improvement of collective farm lands carried out by construction organizations will be included in the plans for
contract work. [12]

It is interesting to note the contrast between the attitude
toward collective farms implicit in the above framework for
investment in land improvements and that expressed by
Khrushchev a year prior to his retirement. At that time,
Khrushchev said, "Of course, state farms should be formed
on tracts newly put under irrigation."[13] In another speech,
he commented "I think that state farm production should be
set up on this irrigated land. State farms are state enterprises. They are better administered. There would be more
confidence that capital investments were being used rationally."[14] With Khrushchev's retirement, the emphasis had
clearly shifted from a program aimed only at state farms to
a program covering both state and collective farms. The
Soviet government desired large-scale investment throughout
the agricultural sector and to achieve this goal it was willing
to assist the collective farms financially.

A more recent campaign has focused on the prevention
of soil erosion. Early in 1967, the CPSU Central Committee
and the U.S.S.R. Council of Ministers decreed that, during
the 1968-1970 period: forest shelter belts should be created
on 324,000 hectares; soil-protecting crop rotation, contour
plowing, grass planting, and similar measures should be
implemented on 324,000 hectares of marginal land; steep slopes
of over 89,000 hectares should be terraced; and an estimated
188 million rubles should be spent on flood-control equipment.[15] Both state and collective farms are to engage in
such activities. Decrees concerning this program include a
new aspect, however. The U.S.S.R. State Bank is to play an
important role in providing credit for expenditures on necessary equipment; and the need to repay the banking system will,
it is expected, encourage a greater concern for improving the
effectiveness of investment.

Agriculture in the U.S.S.R., probably more than agriculture in any other country, has experienced major disruptions

of its investment and production practices. Such disruptions
occurred under both Stalin and his successors. For example,
since 1950 the mergers of collective farms, the advocacy of
the grassland system, the rapid settlement of the Virgin Lands,
the abolition of the Machine Tractor Stations (MTS), implementation of the corn program, rapid expansion of the use of
chemical fertilizer, and the repeated shifts in the agricultural
planning and administrative framework all indicate that the
Stalin-Khrushchev system of government did not foster gradual
change. In his book, Conflict and Decision-making in Soviet
Russia, Sidney Ploss has written:

> Malenkov, and Khrushchev after him, had to seek to
> achieve their major goals through resort to persua-
> sion and intrigue within a structure of diffused power.
> At the same time, other leaders had the right to ex-
> press personal dissent and, most important, the capa-
> bility to marshall support for opposing viewpoints.
> The general effect of this systematized competition
> for personal prestige and sovereignty of ideas was the
> creation willy-nilly of "checks and balances" in the
> mechanics of government. [16]

Such checks and balances have existed, however, only in the
mechanics of deciding which particular policies should be
adopted. Checks and balances have not existed in the implementation of a policy once it has been officially adopted. It
is true that such a policy could later be criticized and reversed,
but such reversals have taken the form of renunciations rather
than moderate revisions. The agricultural scene has been
marked by deliberations over a policy, either complete
acceptance or complete rejection of that policy, then the
rapid, widespread, and large-scale implementation of an
accepted policy, and finally either the continuation or large-
scale rejection of a policy.

> Every day life teaches us that the successful solution
> of the problems confronting us requires fewer loud
> phrases, less campaigning spirit, and more respon-
> sibility. It requires the ability to examine circum-
> stances calmly, to gauge realistically the possibilities
> as well as the difficulties, the successes as well as
> the shortcomings, without hypnotizing oneself with
> resounding words. [17]

In the above quotation, Brezhnev indicates that discussion and
implementation of government policy has not been satisfactory.
Decentralization of decision making may lead to a radically
different type of innovation process. If each farm is free to

decide the extent to which it will adopt a new kind of investment or crop structure, then any shifts may be considerably
more gradual than they have been in the past. Experimentation
with new techniques may involve a smaller proportion of agricultural resources, and failures may not be as extensive.
Decrees concerning irrigation and drainage and also those
dealing with prevention of soil erosion have not yet focused
on this aspect of decentralization; and the reformed planning
framework as it exists today may be criticized for this lack
of emphasis.

SHORTCOMINGS IN INTERENTERPRISE PLANNING

The Soviet government has not committed itself to an
immense program of drainage and irrigation. The land area
in the U.S.S.R. improved by such investment is to increase
from the 1965 level of 15 million hectares to a level of 37
to 39 million hectares (20 per cent of the total sown area) in
1975. By 1970, the midpoint of this ten-year period, the
total figure is supposed to have reached 24 million hectares.
Already this program has encountered the same types of
difficulties experienced by the chemical fertilizer program.
Machinery and equipment have been deficient in respect to
quality. Breakdowns occur too often; spare parts are not
available; and some machinery and equipment provided for
irrigation and drainage projects has not been appropriate for
the necessary tasks. In addition, the workers who have
built the irrigation and drainage networks have not been concerned with the quality of their work; farms complain often
of poor quality construction. Once land has been improved,
it has not been cared for adequately. Central planners have
not been able to control its use effectively, and farms have
lacked local specialists capable of making appropriate decisions. In general, planning has failed in regard to gathering
and analyzing information and coordinating the efforts of the
various enterprises involved. In the face of such shortcomings,
the framework of decentralized responsibility with direct
relationships among the relevant sectors and legally binding
contracts provides an appealing alternative to the past method
of planning.

It must be said that there are serious shortcomings
in both the construction and the utilization of irrigation systems. The Nevinnomyssk Canal was built
fifteen years ago. It is a large, modern installation

with a flow of seventy-five cubic meters of water per second. But its effect is not great . . . The situation is the same with the Prikumsk Canal and the Rostov irrigation system.

The total intake of water for irrigation needs in the U.S.S.R. today amounts to 100 billion cubic meters, but approximately half of this water is lost through seepage. Therefore Comrade N. S. Khrushchev is profoundly right when he speaks of the importance of constructing irrigation systems with lined channels and pipes. We need standard plans for building irrigation systems using reinforced concrete.[18]

Criticism of the design, planning, and construction of land-improvement projects--expressed in 1963 by the director of the U.S.S.R. Ministry of Agriculture's Water Resources Administration--has been repeated often. For example, in a Pravda article, Yu. Pavlovsky and Ye. Grigoryev have noted construction errors due to poor technical documents of the design institutes. "Investigation has revealed that shortcomings in planning remain among the major factors retarding the pace of reclamation work."[19] In a speech in June, 1966, Brezhnev emphasized a coordination problem in this regard and suggested the transfer of entire design organizations and leading individual specialists in this area directly to the U.S.S.R. Ministry of Land Reclamation and Water Resources.[20] Brezhnev hoped through such an administration reorganization to bridge the gap between scientists and designers on the one hand and those responsible for constructing specific projects on the other.

In connection with the drainage and irrigation program, it is necessary to construct huge reservoirs and dams--often in conjunction with hydroelectric projects--as well as to build canals and ditches and to lay tile in the fields. This necessary construction is not simple; it requires workers trained and experienced in this specialty. Hence, the government has had to improve and expand this section of the construction industry with the creation of many new organizations throughout the country. New machinery and equipment must be designed and manufactured for these projects. In 1966 the U.S.S.R. minister of land reclamation and water resources could write that much of the equipment supplied to construction projects was obsolete and of low productivity. "The decisions on the designing of new highly productive continuous-operation rotary earth-moving machines" for example, "are being fulfilled unsatisfactorily and with long delays."[21] The watering

of crops is only in the initial stages of mechanization.
Alekseveysky notes that at least 50 million man-days are
spent in the U.S.S.R. each year on manual watering, so
that if the irrigation program is to be most efficient, substantial progress must be achieved in the development of
sprinkler systems. Even Brezhnev has stated:

> The personnel of the industrial ministeries and
> the enterprises will have to resolve many im-
> portant questions linked with supplying agricul-
> ture with the necessary machinery, equipment,
> and materials. We await from the industrial
> ministries and the research and design organiza-
> tions both serious improvements in the existing
> machines and equipment and the creation of new,
> modern designs. [22]

The gap between construction workers and the farms has
also caused difficulty. As the following quotation indicates,
the reform movement has not yet reached a final set of regulations in this regard, but dissatisfaction with past relationships is **extensive** enough to motivate further experimentation:

> Reclamation workers bear no responsibility for
> the quality of work on land turned over for use.
> They have only one concern--to hand over hec-
> tares to the collective and state farms; what will
> grow on these hectares or whether anything will
> grow at all seems to have nothing to do with them.
> In this connection, some practical workers believe
> it would be useful to make the land-reclamation
> agencies themselves responsible for growing the
> first harvest on drained areas and only after this
> to determine their remuneration for land reclama-
> tion. Then they would have a material interest
> in high-quality work. By the way, this practice
> has already been introduced and has proved quite
> valuable among our neighbors the Lithuanians. [23]

How to utilize most effectively that land which has been
irrigated or drained poses another vital problem for the
U.S.S.R. Chapter 4 will include discussions of the broad difficulty of improving general farming practices through the transfer to the countryside of those ideas developed by modern agriculture science. The present educational system has been
criticized severely for its failure to provide capable agricultural specialists. It is interesting to consider such criticism
in regard to one particular aspect of agricultural science:
utilization of land radically altered through the land-improvement program and proper care and use of the new drainage
and irrigation systems. S. M. Alpatyev, Director of the

Ukraine Hydrotechnology and Reclamation Research Institute,
stated at an agricultural conference:

> We still have not learned to make correct use of
> irrigated land. We have few specialists who are
> well acquainted with irrigation farming and are
> truly enthusiastic about it. The graduates of our
> higher agricultural schools do not have the nec-
> essary knowledge for working on irrigated land.[24]

In regard to the general land-improvement program, Khrushchev stated at the same conference:

> What is the first thing to which we must give our
> attention? The training of people, cadres. Com-
> rades who have spoken here have already brought
> up this important question. With full justification
> they have expressed concern about the fact that
> we are turning out few reclamation and irrigation
> workers. A number of educational institutions
> that used to graduate these cadres have been closed
> for one reason or another. These institutions must
> be reopened and the preparation of irrigation spe-
> cialists must be expanded.[25]

In February, 1964, the Plenary Session of the CPSU
Central Committee urged a substantial reorganization of the
educational system in an effort to overcome the inadequacies
in this area of specialists trained in agricultural science.
The Plenary Session resolved:

> To charge the U.S.S.R. State Planning Committee,
> the U.S.S.R. Ministry of Agriculture, and the
> U.S.S.R. Ministry of Higher and Specialized Second-
> ary Education with devising measures for the train-
> ing and refresher training of cadres for agriculture
> with higher and secondary qualifications, particu-
> larly specialists in chemicalization and irrigation,
> and submitting these measures for the examination
> of the government. To consider it an urgent task
> to carry out in the next few years the transfer of
> all agricultural educational institutions and re-
> search institutes from the cities to state-farm
> bases in order to bring about a radical improve-
> ment in the training of agricultural cadres and to
> strengthen the ties of higher and specialized ed-
> ucational institutions and research institutions
> with production.[26]

Over two years later the Plenary Session of the CPSU
Central Committee was still deeply concerned with the pro-
blem of effective use of irrigation and drainage systems.
In May, 1966, it proclaimed:

The scientific institutions are still developing research in land reclamation weakly. Insufficiently
thorough study is given to questions linked with the
economic substantiation of the order of priorities
in implementing reclamation construction and de-
vising the necessary procedures for the rational use
of drained and irrigated land. Work on the creation
of high-yield varieties of farm crops for such land
is conducted poorly, new reclamation machinery
is being designed too slowly, and altogether inadequate application is being made of the achievements
of science and technology, as well as of the experience of leading farms.[27]

V. V. Matskevich, U.S.S.R. Minister of Agriculture,
in a general review of past Soviet agricultural policies and
an outline of such future policies emphasized this problem of
adopting more effective production techniques:

Developing and introducing a production technology
to provide all kinds of agricultural products, a technology that would correspond to the development of
science and engineering and would be equal to the
tasks of intensive farming, are important in the
struggle to increase crop yields. This applies
primarily to areas where drainage and irrigation
will be carried out on a large scale. As practice
has shown, land reclamation has been carried out
on an inadequate scale and not as a unified complex. Nor have the necessary measures been taken
to introduce modern technology. Owing to this, the
great expenses that reclamation work has entailed
have not been compensated by higher crop yields in
a number of cases.[28]

How can each ruble invested in improving the land be
made more effective? Much of the Soviet discussion of this
question concerns organizational changes--changes which
seek to alter the present system of planning and administration.
Some specific alterations--those seeking to improve the functioning of the research, design, construction, and educational
institutions--have already been mentioned. Perhaps the
most important focus of discussions concerns the questions
of who should be held responsible for the economic effectiveness of investments and how should such economic effectiveness be measured. These questions really underlie most of
the above discussion concerning land improvement--just as
they underlie this book as a whole. Improving practices of
·design, construction and manufacture of machinery and equipment, and, finally, utilization of the improved land all rest

to a major degree on authority over and responsibility for a project and then evaluation of the success of that project.

Of a more general nature is the question of the relation between the state or collective farm and the new investment project. Should the farm as a whole be rewarded for increases in production resulting from the project? On what formula should their extra reward be based? Should the farm pay interest or rent charges to the government for the use of the project? What framework will instill in the farm workers the greatest incentive to utilize the investment most effectively? As indicated above, Khrushchev's answer to some of these questions was to recommend that only state farms be formed on the improved land. Since nearly all the worker's income on such a farm is of a fixed nature, the question of distributing extra income due to the project was not as pressing as it was on a collective farm where the workers would automatically share any increases in farm income. Yet even on a state farm the problem of incentives to stimulate extra thought and effort in utilizing the investment is of great importance. As has already been emphasized, these questions permeate current Soviet economic thought and also practical political deliberations dealing with all aspects of the Soviet economy.

NOTES

1. N. S. Khrushchev, Pravda (October 1, 1963), pp. 1-2.

2. Ibid.

3. Plenary Session of the CPSU Central Committee, Pravda (February 16, 1964), pp. 1-2.

4. K. K. Shubladze, Pravda (September 29, 1963), pp. 1-2.

5. Ibid.

6. L. I. Brezhnev, "On Urgent Measures for the Development of Agriculture in the U.S.S.R.," Pravda (March 27, 1965), pp. 2-4; as translated in The Current Digest of the Soviet Press, XVII, 12, 3.

7. "Directives of the Twenty-third Congress of the CPSU for the Five Year Plan for the Development of the U.S.S.R. National Economy in 1966-1970," Pravda (February 20, 1966), pp. 1-6; as translated in The Current Digest of the Soviet Press, XVIII, 8 (1966), 3.

8. L. I. Brezhnev, "Land Reclamation Is a Fundamental Problem" Pravda (May 28, 1966), pp. 1-2.

9. Ye. Ye. Alekseveysky, Pravda (May 28, 1966), pp. 3-4.

10. Central Committee CPSU, "On the Broad Development of Land Reclamation," Pravda (May 28, 1966), p. 1.

11. L. I. Brezhnev, "Report at the Plenary Session CPSU," Pravda (March 27, 1965), pp. 2-4.

12. "Resolution of the CPSU Central Committee and U.S.S.R. Council of Ministers," Pravda (April 20, 1965), p. 1.

13. N. S. Khrushchev, Pravda (September 29, 1963), pp. 1-2.

14. N. S. Khrushchev, Pravda (October 1, 1963), pp. 1-2.

15. Resolutions of the CPSU Central Committee and U.S.S.R. Council of Ministers, "On Urgent Measures for Protection of the Soil from Wind and Water Erosion," Pravda (April 2, 1967), pp. 1 and 3.

16. Sidney Ploss, Conflict and Decision-making in Soviet Russia (Princeton, New Jersey: Princeton University Press, 1965), p. 278.

17. L. I. Brezhnev, Pravda (November 2, 1966), p. 1.

18. K. K. Shubladze, Director of the U.S.S.R. Ministry of Agriculture's Water Resources Administration, at a Conference of Agricultural Workers of the Northern Caucasus, Pravda (September 29, 1963), pp. 1-2.

19. Yu. Pavlovsky and Ye. Grigoryev, Pravda (November 24, 1966), p. 1.

20.   L. I. Brezhnev, _Pravda_ (May 28, 1966), pp. 1-2.

21.   Ye. Ye. Alekseveysky, U.S.S.R. Minister of Land Reclamation and Water Resources, _Pravda_ (May 28, 1966), pp. 3-4.

22.   L. I. Brezhnev, "Land Reclamation," _Pravda_ (May 28, 1966), pp. 1-2.

23.   G. Lashkevich, _et al._, "Give the New Field a Guarantee of Fertility," _Pravda_ (February 14, 1968), p. 2; as translated in the _Current Digest of the Soviet Press_, XX, 7 (1968), 33-34.

24.   S. M. Alpatyev, _Pravda_ (October 1, 1963), pp. 1-2.

25.   _Ibid._

26.   "On the Intensification of Agricultural Production--Resolution of the Plenary Session of the CPSU Central Committee," _Pravda_ (February 15, 1964), pp. 1-2.

27.   "On the Broad Development of Land Reclamation-Resolution of the Plenary Session of the CPSU Central Committee," _Pravda_ (May 28, 1966), p. 1.

28.   V. V. Matskevich, U.S.S.R. Minister of Agriculture, "New Phase in the Development of Socialist Agriculture," _Voprosy istorii CPSU_, 8, (1966), 3-15.

CHAPTER **4** FARM MACHINERY
AND EQUIPMENT

SHORTCOMINGS IN INTERENTERPRISE PLANNING

The agricultural production process in the U.S.S.R.
today cannot be understood in isolation from the industrial
production process. To increase the effectiveness of farm
machinery and equipment requires not only an improvement
in its utilization, but also an improvement in the manufacture
of that machinery and equipment. In the latter sphere,
Soviet observers--economists, politicians, and farm workers--
are unanimously and intensely dissatisfied with the present
performance of Soviet industry. Discussing farm machinery
and equipment, they emphasize problems in scientific research and design which result in capital goods whose effectiveness is needlessly limited. They criticize the gap between
those responsible for innovation and those who must use the
results of that innovation. Machinery and equipment seem
to break down more often than they should because of their
inferior quality, while spare parts are difficult to obtain and
repair facilities are insufficient. Discussions of farm machinery and equipment often criticize the lack of specialists.
The financing of agricultural investment has received much
attention in the past few years and, with this, the question
of who should make and be responsible for investment decisions. Here the discussion of profit has placed new emphasis
on the formation of prices, both for agricultural produce and
also for those inputs which the farms purchase from the
industrial sector.

For those engaged in agricultural production, each of
these questions is of major importance. Each has been discussed already in connection with the chemical fertilizer and
land improvement programs and each will be again considered
in the second part of the book; for, as has been emphasized,
these problems permeate the Soviet economy. Their pre-
sentation in this chapter, therefore, will be limited to the

specific manner in which they reveal themselves to farm
workers. Numerous examples will be cited to illustrate
how farm workers have been made aware of these problems.
In addition, this chapter will present investment questions
whose relevance is restricted to the farm. For example,
the desire to increase consumption of perishable foods has
faced difficulties in the sphere of transportation and storage
facilities. The decision has been made to create specialized
fruit and vegetable farms near the large urban centers to
help overcome this deficiency. In addition, many have urged
the creation and expansion of processing factories on the farms.
This concept of industry on the farm may also have received
support because of technological unemployment resulting
from the rapid increase in the mechanization of farm tasks.
This unemployment problem seems to be particularly important on collective farms where, unlike the state farms, each
member of the labor force possesses an inherent right to
remain on the farm and share the agricultural produce.

Let us look first at the development of better-quality
machinery and equipment. The Virgin Lands campaign,
initiated in 1954, has encountered severe difficulties due to
wind erosion and the creation of dust bowls similar to those
of the western United States in the 1930's. The newly settled
lands, in Siberia, Kazakhstan, and eastern parts of the
R.S.F.S.R. receive less precipitation than do the areas traditionally cultivated, and this has necessitated the development of
new farming techniques capable of dealing successfully with
such an environment. An important aspect of this adaptation
is the manufacture of new machinery and equipment. The
regular moldboard plow penetrates to a depth of 25 to 27
centimeters, and it buries the stubble that remains in the
fall after the crop has been harvested. The stubble, however,
can be useful in a climate like that of the Virgin Lands. It
helps to ensure the accumulation and even distribution of snow
in the fields. The snow provides moisture in spring and,
together with the roots of the stubble, tends to prevent the
strong winds from blowing the otherwise loose topsoil. Hence
shallow plowing is desirable; but this necessitates the development of new types of equipment.

In 1963, nine years after the eastward migration began,
the chairman of the Virgin Land Territory Farm Machinery
Association and the deputy director of the All-Union Grain
Research Institute emphasized that:

    Models of these machines exist, have undergone tests,
    have gained approval and are recommended for mass

> production. However, the state and collective farms
> are not receiving them . . . The whole trouble lies
> in the unwieldiness of the planning and supply ap-
> paratus and the uncoordinated state of research
> and design forces.[1]

A major gap has existed in the innovation process--the farmers
know what they need, but the industrial suppliers have been
unable or unwilling to provide the appropriate equipment. In
January, 1963, the October Revolution Plant in Odessa had
begun production of the KPL-3-150 flat-cut cultivator. An
improved model, the KP-250, had been subjected to experimental work, as had the GPK-2.5 tiller plow. The Siberian
Farm Machinery Plant had begun to manufacture the LDS-4
shallow-plow seed drill appropriate for sowing on land cultivated without moldboards. However, nearly three years
later several professors could note that "as yet only a small
part of the arable land is being cultivated with implements
required for shallow plowing."[2]

The President of the V. I. Lenin All-Union Academy of
Agricultural Sciences has stated: "The principal consumer
of the products of tractor and farm-machinery building--
agriculture and its guiding agencies--in practice has been cut
off from participation in the creation of new equipment."[3]
The development of machinery and equipment appropriate for
the soil and climatic conditions of the Virgin Lands illustrates
how important this innovation gap has been for Soviet agriculture. The January, 1961, Plenum of the Central Committee of the CPSU attempted to bridge this gap by the creation
of an All-Union Farm Machinery Association which was to
perform several vital tasks: supervision of mechanization
and the development of new equipment and techniques, operation of a network of machine-testing stations, and organization
of the servicing and repair of farm machinery and equipment.
Three years later, the chairman of a collective farm described the functioning of this new organization with very
bitter words:

> The collective farms' equipment operators are
> seriously concerned about the unsatisfactory work
> of the All-Union Farm Machinery Association. The
> leaders of the Farm Machinery Association have no
> sense of responsibility for the technical condition
> and operation of the collective farms' machines
> and tractors. The Farm Machinery Association's
> officials are either only vaguely or not at all
> aware of the state of affairs on the collective farms;
> the supply of spare parts is extremely poor; the

mechanization of labor-intensive processes, especially in animal husbandry, gets almost no attention.[4]
This chairman claimed that the machines sent to the farms
sometimes lacked components and often lacked recent improvements, and he stated openly: "It is time to stop pushing
equipment that no one has ordered. It is necessary to study
demand and to sell those machines for which we have an acute
need."[5]

Recognizing these shortcomings, the U.S.S.R. Council
of Ministers adopted a resolution, in April 1965, to

expand direct ties between collective and state
farms and industrial enterprises and trade organizations, making it possible to lower procurement
costs, to speed up the delivery of products to the
consumer, and to raise the quality of agricultural
products procured.[6]

Recent discussions of planning and administrative reforms
have stressed the concept of direct ties between economic
organizations when one is supplying the other with manufactured
goods. Exactly what form such direct ties should take is still
being debated. Do representatives of each side simply meet
regularly to exchange information? Are specific contracts
to be signed between the two organizations, with inclusion of
detailed descriptions of the goods to be purchased? Are
violations of such contracts to be punished? And, will the
punishment be strong enough to prevent those infractions
which the supplier is tempted to make in order to reduce his
costs? Is the purchasing organization to be free to move to
an alternative supplier if it is dissatisfied with the latter's
products? Will price flexibility be permitted to compensate
each side for changes in quality--and who will decide in
which direction and by how much prices should be changed?
Although such questions have not yet received definite answers,
it is within this sphere of direct contacts that the Soviet leadership today sees the solution to bridging the innovation gap
which exists throughout the Soviet economy.

The problem of innovation is considered here as part of
the general problem of the quality of machinery and equipment
produced by a firm. The above questions concerning direct
contacts between purchaser and supplier are relevant in regard to many aspects of quality. An October, 1966, article
has noted:

Several years ago "Standard Safety Requirements
for Agricultural Machinery and Tools" were
adopted . . . What if the firm does not take the

strict paragraphs of the "Requirements" into
consideration? How will the violator pay for
this? He will not. Often, a safety inspector
participating in the testing of a new machine gives
it a failing mark, but the machine is produced all
the same. [7]

To set specific engineering standards and then to enforce
these does not seem to be an easy task. Who is best qualified--
by virtue of knowledge and objectivity--to decide upon required
specifications? Two men whose work involves this problem
have stated:

One cannot ignore the question of the local staffs'
setting standards of reliability of goods. Today
no one coordinates the work of the thousands of
these staffs which have been set up at individual
industrial enterprises, design bureaus, and research institutues . . . One should not be sur-
prised that the work of these important staffs is
far from effective and that in practice they are
frequently turned into yet another scapegoat, to
be blamed for the low quality and unreliability
of manufactured articles. [8]

Hence these writers have urged that some committee--the
U.S.S.R. State Committee on Standards and Product Quality,
in particular--be responsible for coordination of the setting
of standards.

In an article on this subject, I. Karpenko has stated:
"It is true that standards must be raised legislatively. However, unless there is broad participation in the struggle for
quality by the enterprise collectives themselves, it will be
inappropriate to expect success. "[9] Enforcement is an
ubiquitous and sturdy obstacle in this sphere. He points out
that even when quality inspectors are members of an independent department in a firm, still they may face psychologi-
cal and even monetary punishment if they reject much of the
firm's output because it fails to meet state standards. The
rush in completing goods at the end of the month presents
especially difficult problems for inspectors. The solution
suggested by Karpenko is that inspectors should receive
bonuses based only on the quality of their firm's production
where, for example, the amount of goods returned to the
factory because of faulty construction is used as an index.

Russia's profit reforms have introduced an alternative
approach to this problem of ascertaining which products are
of poor quality. The focus has shifted from inspectors working within the factory to an examination of customer complaints

as they arise. With the decentralization reforms currently
in force, contracts between suppliers of farm machinery and
the farm units have increased greatly in importance, and
fines can be levied against the producer for violations of
specified quality. Such fines accrue to the customer. With
material rewards geared towards its profit, the customer
will, it is expected, eagerly prosecute its suppliers for
delivery of poor quality products.

Numerous writers have urged that fines be raised substantially to make this approach more effective. At the end
of 1967, the U.S.S.R. Council of Ministers adopted these
suggestions: Henceforth, deliveries of output that do not
meet specifications will result in fines of 20 per cent of the
value of the merchandise. Late delivery is to receive similar
treatment: for delays of less than ten days, the fine is 3 per
cent; for delays of more than ten days, the fine is 8 per cent.[10]
Within this new environment, the need for legal advice has
increased. One writer has claimed that collective and state
farms have concluded contracts disadvantageous to themselves because of their ignorance concerning the law, and he
has urged that some lawyers should receive special training
in such matters and should devote their time fully to the legal
problems of state and collective farms.[11]

Let us briefly examine the quality-innovation problem
from the view of the supplier of farm machinery. What is
the result if profit maximization is emphasized and a firm
does strive to innovate and to adhere rigorously to those
quality standards which have been established? The case of
the Dzherzhinsky Tractor Plant in Volgograd illustrates that
this recommendation can lose in practice much of the advantage it seems to possess in theory. Recently this factory
introduced the DT-75 tractor to replace the DT-54 model
previously produced. The chief engineer has written:

> As long as our plant was producing the DT-54 trac-
> tor, it was highly profitable. Profits annually ex-
> ceeded 20 million rubles. More than one million
> rubles were transferred annually into the enter-
> prise's fund, making it possible regularly to pay
> workers substantial bonuses and to allot fixed
> sums of money for housing and cultural and every-
> day construction. But as soon as the plant set
> about the reconstruction of production and began
> to prepare for manufacturing the new tractor, its
> technological and economic indices immediately
> began to take a turn for the worse. The enter-
> prise's fund began to "melt away." The payment

of bonuses was reduced to nearly one-fourth the
previous figure. For all practical purposes, we
are now without an enterprise fund. [12]

In this case of the Dzherzhinsky Tractor Plant, the labor
turnover--particularly that of highly skilled workers--in-
creased sharply and according to the chief engineer the workers are much less concerned about performing their tasks
with creative diligence. Why should profits--and consequently
bonuses--have fallen so suddenly? Skrebtsov criticizes the
prices established for the new tractors.

Quite often prices are established by administrative procedure, without any kind of economic
calculations. It was precisely by such a "method"
that the U.S.S.R. State Planning Committee's
Bureau of Prices determined the value of the DT-75
tractor. [13]

The calculations performed by firm employees were rejected
in this price determination. Skrebtsov claims that two factors
should influence the price to be set for a new good or a
product whose quality has been improved--the expenditures
required to master the new production techniques and to
produce the new good and also the "anticipated economic
effectiveness" of the new or improved good. The precise
manner in which supply-and-demand considerations should
interact in price formation is not analyzed explicitly by him.
This question of the factors that should underlie the price of
any good still forms an area of uncertainty in Soviet economic
thought. Yet it is an extremely important question--the entire concept of profit maximization and the practical decisions
based on this concept can be altered radically by different
assumptions concerning the proper basis for prices.

In connection with farm machinery and equipment, rural
electrification deserves special mention. A. Savinykh, Vice-
Chairman of the U.S.S.R. State Production Committee for
Power and Electrification, stated in 1965 that at that time
only 8 per cent of Soviet collective farms had electric power
even for the illumination of production premises. Only 26
per cent of the country's cows were milked electrically. Even
the provision of water for livestock was not mechanized in
most of the country. [14] The All-Union Farm Machinery Association described above is responsible, together with certain
industrial producers, for the design, manufacture, delivery,
installation, and adjustment of the equipment necessary for
rural electrification. Yet:

No sooner do the electrical lines and facilities go
into operations than they go out of commission . . .
This happens first of all because the electrical
networks and substations in rural localities are
still in poor technical condition. Meanwhile, the
U.S.S.R. State Planning Committee is not providing even minimal resources for performing
repair and operational jobs in the countryside.
And what is the result? Transmission lines into
the collective and state farms are out of order
almost everywhere. [15]

The administrative position of the author of this passage
should lead us to consider the above analysis closely. A.
Savinykh has criticized the shortage of specialists skilled
in rural electrification--a shortage which has hampered not
only installation, but also necessary repairs. Suddenly faced
with a power failure, the farm's labor organization is harm-
fully disrupted as workers are forced to alter their planned
activities and resume the milking and watering of livestock
and other jobs whose mechanization rural electrification had
permitted.

The availability of spare parts, repair facilities, and
skilled technicians capable of executing necessary repairs is
of major importance not only in regard to electrical equipment, but also for the efficient utilization of all that machinery
and equipment used by a farm. Commenting upon the agricultural situation to the Plenary Session of the CPSU Central
Committee, Brezhnev in 1965 stated:

Above all, we must strengthen the repair base of
agriculture. This is a very important question
and we cannot postpone its solution . . . The present repair base makes it possible to implement
only 60 per cent of the necessary repairs in good
time and with high quality. Almost 13,000 farms
lack workshops capable of carrying out even rou-
tine repairs. [16]

A Pravda article in April, 1966, noted that "more than 2
billion rubles are spent annually on the repair of farm machinery in our country. Still, farms often get poorly repaired
machinery back from the workshops. "[17]

Because of this situation, the suggestion often has arisen
that large, specialized repair enterprises should be built to
service a number of farms, each of which independently would
not be large enough to support such enterprises. The Machine
and Tractor Stations were supposed to fulfill this function, but
their dissolution in 1958 caused disruption of the repair system. [18] The All-Union Farm Machinery Association, one of

whose purposes since its formation in 1961 has been to organize an efficient agricultural repair base, has been criticized
severely for its activity in this regard.[19] Writers discussing
this feel that the links between the individual farms and the
Farm Machinery Association are not such as to foster diligence
and concern on the part of the latter organization. With the
reforms, such critics foresee a greater authority and independence within each farm and, because of this, a situation
where such links with a repair organization will rest on a
mutually advantageous basis and on voluntary, jointly negotiated contract obligations. Such obligations may include a
guarantee of reliable operation for a specified time period.[20]
Legal contracts would compel the personnel of the Farm
Machinery Association to bear responsibility for meeting the
repair deadlines vital for successful agricultural production.
In addition, the new emphasis on economic accountability
may encourage more rational decisions in regard to repairs.
The Vice-Chairman of the Russian Republic's Price Committee
has stated that, in the past, the repair of machinery has
sometimes cost the farms more than would the purchase of
new machinery.[21] An appropriate price structure for repairs
will, it is expected, prevent such anomalies in the future.

    Throughout the Soviet economy, criticism is heard of a
general shortage of spare parts. Those responsible for farm
machinery and equipment voice such criticism often and
vigorously.[22] Frequently one can read reports in the Soviet
press of repair workers adopting the extreme policy of dismantling new machines to obtain necessary spare parts.
Some of the reasons for such a shortage are discussed in a
1965 Pravda article.[23] A large proportion of the spare parts
produced must be returned to the manufacturers because
they are defective and of no use. Parts are usually produced
at the convenience of the firm, so that the time pattern of
delivery does not correspond to the needs of farm workers.
Many firms that fulfill the gross-output plan for spare parts
in rubles are not concerned about the assortment plan, so
that while some parts are available, other equally vital parts
are not available. "To this day, little attention is paid to the
labelling, packing, and delivery in complete sets of spare
parts."[24] Together with careless transportation and storage,
this results in damage as well as the receipt by repair facilities of parts other than those required. It is also possible
that the manufacturing firms find it easier to fulfill their
gross-output plan in rubles by constructing complete units
the gross value of which may have a larger component of
supplies purchased outside the plant and a smaller component
of value added than do spare parts.

A June, 1964, article indicates that in the past this situation may have existed to some extent because of a divergence of opinions among the upper echelons of the Soviet administration. The U.S.S.R. State Planning Committee had rejected a proposal to allocate funds for expanding the production of spare parts. V. Ya. Selifonov, Assistant Chief of this committee's department of machine building, explained this decision with the statement:

> We should expand the production of new machines
> and as quickly as possible write off the old and
> worn-out machines for scrap. New machines are
> more reliable and more productive than repaired
> machines.[25]

Reference is made frequently to the lack of standardized parts--a lack which it is claimed complicates the repair process.

> The lack of a uniform technical policy in the pro-
> duction of means for mechanizing agriculture has
> now led to an unjustified multitude of makes and
> varieties of machine designs.[26]

> The almost complete absence of standarization
> of motor vehicles and their parts has led to an
> enormous growth in the assortment of parts.[27]

Statements like these seem to support an increase in centralized control over the production decisions of machinery manufacturers in order to impose a uniformity of components. If the argument that such uniformity would substantially reduce repair expenditures is valid, then there does seem to be a trade-off between such a policy and the benefits to be gained from the decentralization proposed by.many Soviet writers. In any case, from the above discussion it is clear that for the rural population an extremely important concern is the impact of alternative planning and administrative frameworks on the quality of farm machinery--its durability, effectiveness, and suitability for necessary tasks--and on the availability of spare parts and repair facilities.

In the summer of 1963 a group representing the United States Department of Agriculture visited the U.S.S.R. Upon its return it wrote a report concerning its views on Soviet agriculture. One of its comments was:

> We believe the lack of crop specialization in many
> areas hinders increases in agricultural production.
> The lack of specialization in high yielding crops
> adapted to local areas is to an important extent re-
> lated to the lack of improved systems of marketing

and distribution . . . Little attention has been given
to marketing and distribution problems and their
effect on production specialization in the U.S.S.R.[28]

Most of the rural population sells any surplus from its private
plots of land in stalls rented in the city market place for
varying periods of time. Collective farms sometimes do this
as well. This supplements the state distribution system.
Both channels suffer from a lack of transportation and storage
facilities. Many discussions of pricing policies emphasize
the severe cost disadvantages which farms at any distance
from a city must suffer. Without rapid, cheap, and (in many
cases) refrigerated transportation facilities, specialization
and the longer shipping distances that specialization entails
are not feasible for many agricultural products. A wealthy
American farmer named Garst, who won the respect of
Khrushchev and who commented to Khrushchev on certain
agricultural matters, urged that the U.S.S.R. build more
farm-to-market roads. Khrushchev replied before the Plenary
Session of the CPSU:

Mr. Garst recommends that we build "farm-to-
market" roads. Such a concept is of course a
capitalist one, but it is not devoid of economic
sense even in our socialist conditions. But at
present we cannot set aside in full measure the
capital investment for such construction.[29]

As a result of such reluctance to invest in rural roads,

In certain areas, the majority of our trucks are
unable to move at all along rural roads in the
spring, and tractors have to be used to haul
fertilizers and seed.[30]

Even the chief of the Virgin Land Territory Highway Transport
Administration has commented that "the roads are terrible.
Roads should be built by those who drive on them."[31] As a
result of this situation, truck breakdowns are increased and,
more important, the opportunity to transport farm produce
is restricted and the probability of spoilage on the road is
increased.

P. Serebrennikov has emphasized strongly the extremely
poor character of the Soviet transportation system as it relates to perishable foods. He claims that

In the most advanced capitalist countries, cattle
are transported at the rate of 700 to 800 kilometers
a day. . . in the U.S.S.R. the average annual rate
of transportation of animals by rail is not even 100
kilometers. . . Nor does specially equipped truck
transportation for cattle and fowl exist.[32]

Moreover, railroads have virtually no special equipment for
cattle transport. Because of this situation, he claims that
the physical loss of animal weight in the transportation process is very important. In a Pravda article the editors of
Tselinny krai have stated in reference to the Virgin Land
transportation system:

> According to the most modest estimate, up to 100
> per cent of the live weight of livestock is lost on
> the way due to poor feeding and care. [33]

One idea to help overcome this transportation problem
was to develop state farms in close proximity to cities for
the specific purpose of "specializing" in perishable foods.
In 1958, for example, thirty-five farms in the neighborhood
of Moscow were supposed to be devoted entirely to the production of vegetables and potatoes. A Moscow Potato and
Vegetable Trust was established to manage the farms and to
sign contracts for future deliveries to the city of specified
amounts of good quality products at stated prices. Between
1958 and 1962 a total of 570 specialized vegetable and potato
state farms were established in suburban zones throughout
the Soviet Union. M. Alisov has written "In 1962 these state
farms delivered 1,364,000 tons of vegetables to the state or
23 per cent of the total vegetable procurements for the country
as a whole."[34] He also has mentioned that state farms now
provide Moscow with more than half of its potatoes and vegetables and that procurement of vegetables is now more than
twice as large as in 1953. Nevertheless, this writer still
has noted shortcomings in the government program. He has
claimed that "except for title, these farms were distinguished
in no way from nonspecialized ones." In 1962, he has noted,
plantings of potatoes and vegetables at such farms occupied
only 9.5 per cent of their plowland. Yields, he states, have
been very low.

A. Voronin has stated that in 1958 "17 per cent of the
vegetables produced on collective farms and 13 per cent of the
melons grown were used as fodder."[35] Alisov, in the article
mentioned above, has claimed that 219,000 tons spoiled in the
new trade organizations in 1960 and that the total spoilage
was 566,000 tons. In 1961 this figure rose to 1,208,000 tons.
In each of 1962 and 1963, 25,000 tons of vegetables were fed
to livestock on the "specialized" state farms of Leningrad
Province and more than 60,000 tons on state farms of the
Ukraine. In 1961 more than 15 per cent of the cabbage and
37 per cent of the tomatoes shipped to Moscow were of extremely poor quality. A Key problem underlying this spoilage
is the lack of appropriate storage facilities. In 1961 the

Gosplan called for a massive program of warehouse construction for perishable foods. However, in Moscow, for
example, these plans were only one-tenth fulfilled. The 1962
plans were, in turn, fulfilled only one-quarter. A 1963 report
from Sverdlovsk noted that:

> Last autumn tens of thousands of tons of vegetables
> and potatoes perished here in ill-suited warehouses
> and at railroad stations. This year, however, the
> reception points of the city fruit and vegetable trade
> trust have still made no preparation for storage. . .
> Facts show that the vegetable season has been poorly
> greeted not in the Urals alone. A similar picture
> can be observed in several other cities. In the past
> ten days (in August, 1963), 20,000 tons of spoiled
> tomatoes have been sent as livestock fodder from
> Moscow's Krasnaya Presnya Fruit and Vegetable
> Office. [36]

One possible solution to the problem of spoilage in transportation and storage is to move the food processing industry
to the countryside from its present location in the cities.
This policy of industrialization of the countryside has received
considerable support in recent Soviet articles. This support
is based not only on the belief that spoilage can thereby be
reduced. It is also based on the realization that investment
and technological change are reducing the optimum level of
agricultural employment. "More and more, hands are re-
leased by mechanization. Collective farms open auxiliary
enterprises but the rapid population growth keeps the problem
acute. "[37]

> One of the consequences of rapid technological
> progress is the release of labor . . . Only a very
> insignificant part of the collective farmers partici-
> pate in the work of the auxiliary enterprises at col-
> lective farms and the labor applied there amounts
> to no more than 2 per cent of all labor outlays in
> the rural economy. [38]

Many countries have experienced the dislocation in the
labor market caused by investment and technological change
in agriculture. This problem is intensified in the U.S.S.R.,
however, by the existence of collective farms where the
members of these cooperatives have the right to work as many
hours as they wish, regardless of the productivity of those
hours and also the right to receive an income which is not
based on the marginal product of labor. The collective farm
member cannot be forced to leave the cooperative simply
because the farm's labor requirements have fallen. One

Soviet writer has stated clearly that collective-farm chairmen
have restricted investment because of their inability to find
productive work for the members that such investment would
replace. [39] Most observers strongly recommend the development of industrial enterprises in the countryside to assist in
overcoming this problem and also to provide work for the
general rural labor force during the winter months when farm
workers are, for the most part, unoccupied. [40] However,
this recommendation by itself is not without criticisms.
G. Lisichkin has pointed out that even when several collective
farms pool their resources to construct an industrial enterprise, still they may be forced to build such a small firm
that costs are higher than those of a larger firm enjoying
economies of mass production.

> Remember the intercollective-farm hydroelectric
> stations that were once built, with great enthusiasm
> and at equally great expense. Let their fate after
> the collective farms were hooked up to the state
> power system serve as a background as we discuss
> the correct, economical treatment of intercollective-
> farm construction. [41]

Lisichkin provides the example of 130 collective farms
near Bakhchisarai in the Crimea that contributed funds for
the construction of a plant to provide them with cement which
they were finding difficult to obtain. Legal restrictions prevented Crimean state farms and industrial firms as well as
collective farms outside the administrative "territory" from
contributing toward this construction. Consequently, at this
enterprise the cost of a ton of cement is 11 rubles 32 kopeks,
while at other plants with capacities as much as five times
larger the cost is less than 6 rubles. The current retail
price of 36 rubles a ton ensures success for practically any
such plant, but the 1966-to-1970 plan calls for rapid development of the cement industry. The retail price can be expected
to fall and high cost producers like the Bakhchisarai Combine
may no longer be profitable. In view of such developments,
Lisichkin stresses that industrialization of the countryside
should be conducted with a view towards cost minimization
and with a financial framework that allows construction of
large enough plants to permit cost minimization. Decision
makers should be aware of the price being paid (if any)--in
the form of higher costs for rural than for urban plants--to
permit workers to remain in the countryside and to keep them
occupied in winter months. Emphasis on profitability may
exert a noticeable impact on this particular aspect of agricultural investment.

FINANCING INVESTMENT

It seems appropriate at this point to consider in more
detail the question of financing investment in agriculture. In
the past, the government has given funds to state farms regularly for their general operation. For collective farms,
however, provision of direct financial grants rather than
repayable loans has been exceptional behavior. Collective
farms have been basically self-supporting. They have been
able to remain self-supporting largely because wages have
not been fixed at some predetermined level, but rather have
been paid out of any profits that may remain after all expenses
have been paid. Thus, for collective farms, a bad year or a
farm with poor land or bad management has meant lower
wages rather than more government support. [42] An exception
to this approach has been provided by periodic cancellation
of certain debts owed by the collective farms. In April,
1965, for example, the CPSU Central Committee and U.S.S.R.
Council of Ministers decreed that all indebtedness remaining
from the 1957 sale of MTS equipment, premises, and tools
to the collective farms was now to be cancelled. [43]
    In July, 1966, a basic alteration was made in the financial
framework. The CPSU Central Committee and the U.S.S.R.
Council of Ministers decided that guaranteed minimum wages
should be paid for the labor of collective farm members.

> By this resolution, the collective farms are advised
> to introduce beginning July 1, 1966, guaranteed pay-
> ments (in cash and in kind) for the labor of the col-
> lective farmers, based on the rates of pay of the
> corresponding categories of state farm workers. . .
> The collective farmers are to be given the guaran-
> teed payments for labor in cash not less than once
> a month. [44]

Wages are now supposed to be the first item paid from collective farm earnings. If a farm is unable to meet its wage
payments, the U.S.S.R. State Bank is obligated to lend that
farm the amount it needs for this purpose. [45] This revision
has made it less likely that collective farms will remain
self-supporting. Much depends on the level of wages, cost
of other inputs, and the price of agricultural produce, but
for a farm poor in regard to management, soil, or climate
the wage fund will no longer serve as a buffer to absorb the
cost of other expenses. Now such a farm may find itself
continually increasing the amount of its indebtedness to the

Bank in a manner completely unrelated to its level of investment or stock of capital. This development may be considered
undesirable and so may give rise to additional basic changes.
Hence it seems that, for collective farms, the financial
structure is still in a period of flux.

State farms are also experiencing changes in their
financial structure.

> The amount of profits channeled into the expansion
> of production resources now constitutes an insigni-
> ficant share of total capital investments. In 1963,
> the state farms of the Russian Republic met only 3
> per cent of all capital investments through their own
> resources; the rest came from the state budget.
> Such a practice conceals a substantial shortcoming.
> Inasmuch as no return is expected from the funds al-
> located to the state farms from the budget for build-
> ing accommodations and acquiring equipment, the
> farm leaders have little interest in economizing
> on them. [46]

Because of this lack of incentive to utilize farm capital
effectively, many writers have urged that budget financing
of state farm investments be cancelled and that instead the
government should extend long-term loans. In March, 1965,
Brezhnev stated:

> We must abandon excessive regimentation in the dis-
> tribution of capital investments and subsidies to the
> state farms and shift the state farms to full cost ac-
> counting (khozraschet) as soon as possible. The
> state farms will retain for their own uses the pro-
> fits they recieve. [47]

In 1967, the Soviet government did transfer 390 state
farms to the new framework of economic accountability. They
have had to pay for all production costs and for capital investments other than housing or provision of social and
cultural amenities. They have been encouraged to borrow
from the banking system to meet the costs of investment;
no longer can they receive regular grants from the state
budget. The government agreed to pay these state farms the
same prices it promised the collective farms in 1965. With
this new financial structure, the 390 state farms received new
responsibilities for decision making. The initial decree of
the CPSU Central Committee and the U.S.S.R. Council of
Ministers stressed this greater economic independence and
declared that the number of plan indices requiring the approval
of the bureaucracy should be reduced. [48] This decree also

emphasized the experimental nature of the program and the intention to remain flexible in regard to modification in it. Since 1967, the entire state-farm system has been shifted toward the framework, although suggestions for alterations in the new regulations have appeared. Implications of this new system will be discussed in the general comments of succeeding chapters.

The U.S.S.R. State Bank stands between the central planners and government officials on the one hand and the individual farms on the other. Its role will certainly increase in importance with the implementation of economic reforms that provide for greater decentralization of investment funds allocation. Already it performs more than a passive role in this sphere. In a signal article to which several prominent Soviet writers have replied, G. Lisichkin commented upon several aspects of previous bank practice.

> The principal of providing capital investments according to "a little for everybody" prevents our agriculture from moving forward...Indeed, credit is given in the first place to those who manage production most poorly. This is done under a fine-sounding slogan: "Aid the Lagging."[49]

The view presented by Lisichkin is that in the allocation of investment funds the banking system must seek the greatest possible increase in agricultural output; it must establish priorities based upon the production increase per ruble invested, rather than upon the welfare criterion of aiding the poorest farms.

The state farm reforms discussed above have included the requirement that farms transferred to the new economic conditions should pay interest for the capital they use. The original government decree of 1967 provided for an annual charge of 1 per cent of the value of fixed production assets, excluding livestock and excluding assets paid for out of farm profits. The 1967 decree explicitly stated that this charge was being instituted in order to encourage efficient use of farm capital. On the surface, this goal seems to resemble the investment criterion advocated by Lisichkin in the statement quoted above. Yet the 1967 decree provided that farms whose profitability was less than 25 per cent of total production costs did not have to pay the charge for assets. In any case, the low annual charge of 1 per cent may not have much effect in allocating capital towards the most productive ventures. Critics have recognized this inadequacy and some have advocated an increase in the interest charge to achieve a more effective distribution of investment funds.[50]

In pursuing the goal of the greatest possible increase in total production, however, the bank, according to other writers, must be careful not to intervene arbitrarily in the affairs of each enterprise.

> As time goes by, the bank has turned increasingly into a kind of universal controller. There is not a single question of economic activity to be found to-day that the State Bank does not control. . . We bank officials are unnoticeably but steadily being drawn into purely administrative and managerial functions with respect to the controlled enterprises. . . The State Bank is thereby trying to assume functions that are completely irrelevant to it and beyond its power. No matter how much faith the State Bank board has in the abilities of its local personnel, the latter are still unqualified to perform such tasks. To lay such obligations on them means in fact to compel them to become arbitrary toward the bank clients. [51]

A. Poskonov, the Chairman of the Board of the U.S.S.R. State Bank, has agreed that bank officials should not intervene in the details of enterprise production--details about which they lack the knowledge necessary for such intervention to be beneficial.

> We fully agree that the bank offices should not engage in petty tutelage over enterprises. The State Bank Board does not orient officials of the bank's offices toward this, nor toward "prying into" the technology of production. Yet in everyday practice this defect has not yet been eliminated everywhere. The State Bank is in favor of expanding the rights of enterprises and their economic independence, and for freeing them from petty tutelage on the part of various agencies, including the bank. [52]

The proper role of the banking system in the Soviet economy is not clearly defined. Too much surveillance and control over the daily operations of an industrial or agricultural enterprise is generally condemned as being simply one more form of governmental interference--and perhaps an extremely inefficient form. On the other hand, if bank officials are to ensure that their loans can and will be repaid, then the bank's personnel must be cognizant of many details of the borrower's operations. The power to deny or limit a loan--which the bank does possess--is in itself the power to influence a firm's operations as the latter seeks to become more credit worthy in the eyes of the bank. The role of the

bank in the Soviet economy is a sphere within which major
changes are likely to occur in the near future.

Prior to 1966, farms relied continually on the wholesale
or marketing organizations for financial assistance. The
latter were to provide loans to a farm up to 30 per cent of
the value of output that the farm had contracted to deliver to
the state. For collective farms considered to be financially
weak, this could be raised to 40 per cent. Payments to cover
these loans were then deducted from the collective farms'
accounts at the rate of 60 per cent of the value of each shipment of farm produce. As was noted above, the State Bank
in 1966 was made responsible for providing such loans as
were necessary for collective farms to meet their guaranteed
wage payments, and it appears that the subsidiary financing
by the procurement organizations is now to be shifted entirely
to the banking system. [53]

In order for the banking system to perform those functions
already expected of it and those functions relating to state
farm finance that will be expected of it in the near future, key
changes must be enacted in other sectors of the economy. In
regard to obstacles that the Bank has been facing for some
time, the Vice-Chairman of the Board of the U.S.S.R. State
Bank has emphasized that the bank's role in achieving the
greatest possible increase in production has been severely
limited by the nature of the market for building materials
and equipment. Availability of construction supplies rather
than availability of credit has been the main determinant in
agricultural investment. In each state farm, investment projects are based upon the annual central plan, and finance here
has played basically an accommodating role. Collective
farms, on the other hand, have been left to their own initiative
and luck; and the ability to obtain necessary construction
supplies or skilled workers for any project is not necessarily
related to the advantages of that project or the Bank's priority
rating of that project. [54]

> The collective farm acquires the bricks, cement,
> and lumber wherever and whenever it can. But
> time passes, and the funds allocated go unused. If
> the effectiveness of capital investments on the col-
> lective farms is to be raised, it is necessary to im-
> prove planning and to supply them with materials
> through the same procedure by which the state con-
> struction organizations are supplied. [55]

What Ushakov seems to be suggesting is a framework
within which responsibility for the effectiveness of investment would rest entirely upon the central planners; and the

Bank would only lend the amounts for each farm that the
planners considered necessary. This is one possible direction that change could follow in an effort to develop a framework for the consistent evaluation of agricultural investment
projects. However, this is perhaps not the best direction
nor is it the most likely direction that change will follow.
What is important to note here is that any movement to increase the responsibility of the Bank for investment allocation
cannot be considered in isolation from the market for building
materials, equipment, and labor.

　　Direct contracts between individual enterprises and the
Bank cannot be considered in isolation from the market for
goods and services. In a free competitive market for goods
and services, the impact of this market enters through the
estimated cost of the project; and the only relevant question
is whether the prices of inputs have been estimated realisti-
cally. Here market prices are generally available as a basis
for estimation (although possible changes in these introduce
an element of uncertainty). In a market that is centrally
planned, the wishes and decisions of the planners may enter
either through prices in the same manner as in a competitive
market or, if the planners do not adjust prices so as to clear
the markets, through the rationing decisions of the planners.
In the case of rationing, the link between the bank and the
market becomes much more tenuous. The decisions of the
planners may be different from those of the bankers. Some
firms may have a credit line they cannot use, while other
firms may have access to resources but no credit with which
to pay for them. It is here that inefficiency can become most
apparent. Ushakov is correct in stressing such inefficiency
in the past relationship of central planners, the collective
farm, and the bank; and he is also correct in his belief that
the inefficiency can be overcome by concentrating responsibility for detailed investment allocation on the shoulders of
either the central planners or the bank. His advocacy of the
central planners is more open to criticism, particularly from
the point of view of flexibility in the alteration of plans to
meet changing circumstances throughout the year.

　　G. Lisichkin, an economist near the front of the decentralization movement, has agreed with the view that local decision
making is being hampered by the rationing of necessary equipment and building materials. Farms may borrow credit or
earn profits; but scarcities in the commodity market have
meant that such money cannot be spent. Lisichkin's solution
is to expand the competitiveness of the market for commodities,

freeing it even more from government regulation and ensuring
that the farms with more money can, in fact, purchase more
raw materials and equipment. With this approach, the role
and importance of local bank authorities would be greatly
expanded.[56]

We have noted the feeling among Soviet observers that
state farms should no longer receive free grants from the
government, but rather should be required to repay any funds
provided to them. Ushakov, in the article mentioned above,
has emphasized that for this to be done, changes are again
necessary in sectors outside of the banking structure. The
problem here is that in the past the state farms in the U.S.S.R.
have received total profits that have been far too small to repay within a reasonable time period the total volume of funds
that are being channeled into them. In 1964, for example, the
planned level of profits was only 4.5 per cent of the planned
level of investments for that year (or less than 1 per cent of
the total capital stock on state farms at that time). A shift to
loans and repayments has required, therefore, a considerable
revision of the price structure.

> It is time to solve in practice the question of planning
> the economic effectiveness of capital investments.
> We calculate effectiveness only in the design stage.
> However, when production starts up, this question
> recedes into the background or disappears altogether
> from the view of the economists. One often hears
> that this or that enterprise has not achieved its de-
> signed capacity, but one never hears that it has not
> achieved its designed effectiveness.[57]

The search for an index which reflects the effectiveness with
which capital is currently being utilized has entailed much
discussion of profits. In such discussions, farm profits are
seen as serving not only as the source from which loans may
be repaid; and loan repayment is not seen as the only threat
that inspires most efficient utilization of capital. A farm's
profits are seen also as the source of wage bonuses and
employee fringe benefits; and the latter are expected to provide a constant spur towards improvement. With profits
being granted this new role in the Soviet economy, however,
prices must be revised in a much more drastic manner than
that envisaged by the writer of the above passage whose
central concern was that the current level of state-farm profits was too low to repay loans within a reasonable time period.

If an enterprise is urged, by national leaders and by the
self-interest of its own workers, to maximize its profits,

then each enterprise will seek to alter its pattern of inputs
and outputs as one means of achieving that goal. Belousov
has noted that "under present conditions, the most 'advantageous' product for an enterprise does not always prove to be
the one the national economy needs most. But this is a
shortcoming not of the profits concept but of price formation."[58] The price of each input and each output now becomes
a variable which will definitely affect the production decisions
of the enterprise. Hence, within such a context of profit
maximization, individual prices and the framework for price
formation attain an importance they did not possess under
those methods of central planning traditionally utilized in the
Soviet economy.

NOTES

1. De. Omelyanenko and S. Sdobnikov, "Give the Virgin
Land New Soil Cultivating Machines," Pravda (January 16,
1963), p. 4.

2. Doctors of Economics M. Gendelman and V. Slobodin
and Professor S. Avev, "Place Economic Analysis at the
Basis of Production," Pravda (October 25, 1965), p. 2.
In this regard, see also A. Barayev, Izvestiya (May 31, 1963),
p. 3. A. Zaudalov and V. Blokh, "Plans and Possibilities
of Virgin Land Farming," Pravda (June 15, 1963), p. 2.

3. P. Lobanov, "Science and Standards of Farming,"
Izvestiya (April 1, 1965), p. 3.

4. M. Moiseyev, Chairman of the Young Guard Collective Farm, "Concerns of a Collective Farm Village,"
Kommunist 2 (January, 1964), 58-60.

5. Ibid.

6. U.S.S.R. Council of Ministers, Pravda (April 11,
1965), p. 1.

7. R. Zaitsev, Komsomolskaya Pravda (October 13,
1966), p. 2.

8.   B. Gnedenko, Vice-Chairman of the Scientific
Council of Cybernetics under the Presidium of the U.S.S.R.
Academy of Sciences; and Ya. Sorin, Chairman of the Public
Committee for Reliability and Quality Control under the All-
Union Council of Scientific and Technical Societies, Izvestiya
(July 21, 1964), p. 3.

9.   I. Karpenko, "What Good Means," Izvestiya (July 30,
1965), p. 3.

10.   The U.S.S.R. Council of Ministers, "The Principle
of Mutual Responsibility," Izvestiya (November 15, 1967),
p. 2; P. Bunich and V. Perlamutrov, "The Strength of a
Contract," Pravda (April 3, 1968), p. 2.

11.   G. Dobrovolsky, "The Collective Farm Should Have
a Lawyer," Pravda (April 6, 1968), p. 2.

12.   A. Skrebtsov, "The Plant and the New Machine,"
Pravda (September 15, 1965), p. 4.

13.   Ibid.

14.   A. Savinykh, "Put Electricity into Fields and Livestock Sections," Pravda (September 17, 1965), p. 2.

15.   Ibid.

16.   L. I. Brezhnev, "On Urgent Measures for the Further
Development of Agriculture in the U.S.S.R.," Pravda
(March 27, 1965), pp. 2-4.

17.   V. Kazartsev, Pravda (April 14, 1966), p. 2.

18.   Brezhnev, Op. Cit.

19.   See, for example, V. Yegorushkin and V. Sharov,
Pravda (May 15, 1965), p. 2; A. Karapetyan, Izvestiya (June
12, 1965), p. 3; V. Kazartsev, Pravda (April 14, 1966), p. 2.

20.   A. Boronin, I. Lakhno, and I. Totsky, "The Repair
Industry," Pravda (March 23, 1967), p. 2.

21. N. Dergachev, "The Economic Interrelationships between Collective and State Farms and Industrial Enterprises Require Further Improvement," Pravda (February 4, 1968), p. 2.

22. See, for example, editorials in Pravda (February 13, 1965), p. 1 and Pravda (March 7, 1965), p. 3. See also: A. Andreyev, "The Harvest Cannot Wait," Izvestiya (July 18, 1965), p. 5.

23. B. Gnedenko, A. Bachkirtsev, and V. Popov, "Reliable Machinery Components," Pravda (February 25, 1965), p. 1.

24. Ibid.

25. N. Petrov and I. Totsky, Pravda (June 25, 1964), p. 2.

26. P. Lobanov, President of the V. I. Lenin All-Union Academy of Agricultural Sciences, "Science and Standards of Farming," Izvestiya (April 1, 1965), p. 3.

27. M. Khartsiyev and G. Bazylenko, "What Kind of Motor Vehicles Does the National Economy Need?" Pravda (May 18, 1965), p. 2.

28. Foreign Agricultural Economic Report No. 13, Soviet Agriculture Today (U. S. Department of Agriculture, December 1963), p. 20.

29. N. S. Khrushchev, "Concluding Speech to the Plenary Session," Pravda (December 15, 1963), pp. 1-3.

30. N. Khartsiyev and G. Bazylenko, loc. cit.

31. N. Miller, R. Zhantasov, A. Frolov, I. Kasantsev, A. Pavlov, and A. Andreyev, "Gross Output of Roads," Izvestiya (June 29, 1965), p. 3.

32. Serebrennikov, "Problems of Procurement and Processing of Livestock Products," Problems of Economics (February 1959), p. 42.

33. Editors of Tselinny krai, Pravda (August 5, 1965), p. 2.

34.   M. Alisov, "Urban Potato and Vegetable Shortages: Some Proposals," Kommunist, 15 (October, 1963), 88-95.

35.   A. Voronin, "Combining Agriculture and Industrial Production in the Countryside," Problems of Economics (January, 1962), p. 34.

36.   Izvestiya (September 6, 1963), p. 1.

37.   Yu. Chernichenko, "The Honest Ruble," Pravda (November 20, 1966), pp. 2-3.

38.   M. Vasilenko and S. Kolesnev, "Problems of Utilization of Labor Resources in the Countryside," Kommunist, 18 (1965), 65-74.

39.   G. Radov, "In and Around the Villages," Literaturnaya gazeta (October 18, 1966), pp. 2-3; (October 20, 1966), pp. 1-2

40.   For discussions of this subject and descriptions of the rural enterprises already in operation in addition to the articles already mentioned see: F. Tabeyev, "The Agro-Industrial Complex," Izvestiya (March 4, 1964), p. 3; G. Yarmoshchuk, P. Gumenchuk, V. Prishlyak, Izvestiya (March 19, 1964), p. 1; and P. Kantselyaristov, "Agro-Industrial Complexes in Action," Izvestiya (August 14, 1964), p. 3.

41.   G. Lisichkin, Pravda (September 19, 1966), p. 1.

42.   For a more detailed discussion of this subject see V. V. Matskevich, U.S.S.R. Minister of Agriculture, "Aid to Rural Areas," Izvestiya (December 28, 1965), p. 4; and I. Gustov, "The Bank and the Collective Farm" Pravda (June 20, 1966), p. 2.

43.   Resolutions of the CPSU Central Committee and the U.S.S.R. Council of Ministers, Pravda (April 20, 1965), p. 1.

44.   Resolutions of the CPSU Central Committee and the U.S.S.R. Council of Ministers, "On Raising the Material Incentive of Collective Farmers in the Development of Communal Production," Pravda (May 18, 1966), p. 2.

45. See "Strengthening the Rural Economy," Izvestiya (December 26, 1966), p. 2.

46. L. Kassirov, "Call for a New Farm Price Policy and Profit System" Pravda (January 22, 1965), p. 2.

47. L. I. Brezhnev, "On Urgent Measures for the Further Development of Agriculture in the U.S.S.R.," Pravda, (March 27, 1965), pp. 2-4.
Professors Gregory Grossman and Harold Berman each have written brief articles concerning the meaning of khozraschet. Referring to an article by Nemchinov, Grossman [in The Current Digest of the Soviet Press, XVI, 20 1964] states, "If I understand him correctly, by khozraschet or khozraschetnoye nachalo he means a situation (Principle) where the individual firm conducts its affairs in a business-like way according to certain definite rules and does so in a relatively autonomous fashion."
Professor Berman [in The Current Digest of the Soviet Press, XVI, 23, (1964) 14] has stated, "Khozraschet signifies the responsibility of an economic organization to respond for its liabilities with its assets. A khozraschetny enterprise, as contrasted with a budgetary enterprise, is expected to pay its own way; it cannot normally rely upon reimbursement of its losses by higher economic agencies."
The term khozraschet appears very often throughout the remainder of this book, and so it will be useful to remember the above interpretations.

48. CPSU Central Committee and the U.S.S.R. Council of Ministers, "Concerning the Transition of State Farms and Other State Agricultural Enterprises to Full Economic Accountability," Pravda (April 15, 1967), p. 1.

49. G. Lisichkin, "Credit on Faith or Growth on Credit?" Izvestiya (January 25, 1964), p. 3.

50. See, for example, L. Braginsky, "The Bank and Its Customers," Izvestiya (September 15, 1967), p. 3.

51. M. Breido, Manager of the Leninborough branch of the State Bank Krasnoyarsk, "Why the Financier Replaces the Engineer," Izvestiya (July 22, 1964), p. 3.

52.   A. Poskonov, Chairman of the Board of the U.S.S.R. State Bank, "The State Bank and the Economy," Izvestiya (March 25, 1965), p. 5.

53.   For discussion of this aspect of agricultural finance, see: V. V. Matskevich, U.S.S.R. Minister of Agriculture, "Aid to Rural Areas," Izvestiya (December 28, 1965), p. 4; "Improvement of the System of Extending Credit to Collective Farms," Izvestiya (December 26, 1965), p. 2; I. Gustov, "The Bank and the Collective Farm" Pravda (June 20, 1966), p. 2.

54.   For a description of construction on collective farms, see Yu. Chernichenko, "The Honest Ruble," Pravda (November 20, 1966), pp. 2-3.

55.   V. Ushakov, Vice-Chairman of the Board of the U.S.S.R. State Bank, "Credit, Economy, and Profit," Izvestiya (October 7, 1964), p. 3.

56.   G. Lisichkin, "Two Years after the Reforms," Novy mir, 2, (February 1967), 160-185.

57.   R. Belousov, "The Emphasis Should Be on Economic Effectiveness," Pravda (November 13, 1964), p. 2.

58.   Ibid.

CHAPTER **5** THREE ECONOMIC
FRAMEWORKS FOR
CENTRAL PLANNING

Each nation has developed its own set of specific policies
for government intervention in economic activities. Such a
set of policies can be seen as falling into a planning spectrum,
where its position in the spectrum depends upon the type of
decisions that must be made by central government officials
on the one hand and the type of decisions that must be made
by economic enterprises and local governments on the other.
At one end of the spectrum, central-government officials are
responsible for all the details involved in the operation of each
economic enterprise. At the other end of the spectrum,
central-government officials restrict their intervention to the
determination of broad monetary, fiscal, and tariff policies.
In the center of the spectrum, central planners set different
guidelines, such as prices, for each industry or region but
permit decentralized decision making once the guidelines have
been declared. Each of these three economic frameworks
presents central planners with its own set of problems; and
each set of problems requires the analysis of a particular kind
of economic information.

CENTRALIZATION OF ALL DECISIONS
CONCERNING ECONOMIC ENTERPRISES

The centralization of decisions promises a greater certainty concerning the future course of economic developments.
Without central direction, some industries might produce too
little; and the resultant bottlenecks could restrain progress
throughout the entire economy. Without central direction,
some industries might produce too much; and excessive inventories would accumulate. It is expected that the integration
of current production plans and of future investment projects
will prevent such sectoral underproduction or overproduction.

It is expected that enterprises will expand in the proper proportion; their activities will be synchronized. The government may provide special assistance to enterprises that find themselves in difficulty. It may send more effective management personnel to lagging enterprises, for example. The detailed planning involved in such an economic system could provide for the employment of each citizen. Hence, the danger of an economic depression could be avoided.

Such a planning framework requires that central planners know all the details concerning each production process in the economy, that they coordinate such details, and that they revise their decisions as the production processes change. Can a government be confident that complete and accurate information concerning each production process will, in fact, be transferred from each enterprise--industrial, agricultural, and financial--to its central planners? Even if the central planners can obtain the requisite information, can they reconcile and adjust the production plans of each enterprise so as to achieve the synchronization of all demands for each product with all supplies of each product? These problems of information and coordination are intensified by any change in the circumstances surrounding an enterprise's production process. Any change in such circumstances requires recalculations by the central planners and the issuing of new commands. In practice, can this flexibility be maintained?

The Stakhanovite movement of former years and the widely publicized socialist competition of today testify that even the Russian Communist Party believes an ordinary worker can vary his output significantly merely by working more diligently or more skillfully. How can events of nature such as droughts or floods be truly predicted and accounted for in the plan? If the economy engages in international trade, can the plan not be disrupted by unforeseen changes in export or import prices? One of the most striking features of the Soviet production process as it has operated in the past has been its susceptibility to machinery breakdowns and the difficulties of obtaining spare parts and repairing the equipment. Inevitably plans have been disrupted. A positive relationship exists between slack and decentralized flexibility, on the one hand, and ability to overcome such difficulties smoothly on the other. Soviet leaders have always been reluctant to provide for slack in their planning. After all, should not a perfect plan fit together perfectly? How can inventories of industrial inputs be productive just as inventories? Is growth not being sacrificed by increasing inventories? Decentralized flexibility is limited by this framework. Local enterprise directors cannot alter their production

plans in conformity with the changing features of their environment. Information must travel to the central planners; the
central planners must replan; instructions must go back to the
enterprises. Delay occurs. The inability to forecast any
particular production function precisely and, consequently,
the need for flexibility in planning form a major issue because
in a modern economy one production function is itself an integral part of the production functions of other enterprises.
John Montias has written concerning Poland that "In 1955,
screws and bolts were so short that they were a limiting factor
in the production of boilers--and ships!"[1] Above-plan production can, it is true, be stored as finished inventories, to be
allocated in the next plan. Below-plan production, however,
means that a firm's industrial or agricultural customers will
have their plans disrupted as well.

A modern economy encounters these problems to a greater
extent than does a country in the initial stages of its development. As an economy develops, the degree to which production
processes are interrelated increases due to increasing specialization in making old products and to the development of new
products whose very nature is increasingly complicated and
demands more diverse inputs (the modern aircraft versus the
horse-drawn carriage, for example). Thus the production
processes of a nation's enterprises become increasingly interrelated, and the problem of coordinating all production plans
becomes more difficult. The flexibility problem also becomes
more difficult because an unforeseen development in any one
firm will now affect many other firms in a chain reaction whose
intensity can increase--as from screws to ships. A simple
deterioration of quality or improper assortment of one firm's
output can cause another firm's output to be less useful--or
even completely useless.

Economic development involves the differentiation of commodities. On the production side, machinery and intermediate
products are modified to become more appropriate for the
different tasks they perform. On the consumption side, people
spend their rising incomes on a wider variety of goods. For
the central allocation of commodities, each modification or
variety must be considered as a separate product. The increasing number of items complicates the three problems of
information, coordination, and flexibility. The modern emphasis on quality or appropriateness also adds to these difficulties in that many aspects of quality cannot be quantified
easily. Successful planning requires that precise information
concerning a desired product be conveyed from potential

customers to the central planners. The planners must be able
to compare this information with information concerning the
detailed production possibilities of enterprises that might make
the desired item. Finally, the planners must decide which
firms should make the item, how much should be produced,
and to whom it should be distributed. Involved in this process
is a transfer and analysis of information that can be achieved
most readily in terms of statistics. If blueprints or verbal
descriptions are necessary, as they are with many aspects of
quality, then the transfer and analysis of information are greatly complicated.

Changes in technology that can affect both the quality and
the cost of a product have become prominent features of all
modern economies and appear essential for their progress.
An economically less-developed nation can simply copy the
technology of more advanced countries. As the technology gap
between the former and the latter is closed, however, the
framework for central planning must actively foster quality
improvements and cost reductions if the nation's rate of economic growth is to be maintained. With the centralization of
all decisions concerning the operation of the economy, central
planners must obtain detailed knowledge concerning potential
innovations; and they must be able to ascertain whether, in
fact, the innovations should be implemented.

Hence, as a nation becomes economically advanced, it experiences at least four trends that complicate the information,
coordination, and flexibility problems inherent in the planning
framework where all economic decisions are centralized.
First, products become more complex and require a wider
variety of inputs, so that the production functions of the nation
become increasingly interrelated. Second, both production and
consumption goods are subjected to a growing number of modifications. From the central planners' viewpoint, the number
of items to be considered increases. Third, there is a modern
emphasis on quality or appropriateness, and many such aspects
of a commodity cannot be quantified easily. Fourth, as a nation
nears the forefront of international technology, it must foster
domestic innovation; and the need to obtain and evaluate information concerning potential innovations presents central planners
with an additional complication.

These difficulties may hamper central planning to such an
extent that individual enterprises do in fact make decisions
concerning their operations. The enterprises may violate centrally issued directives without punishment, knowing that the
central authorities are unable to detect such infractions. The

enterprises, for example, may ignore repeated pleas by the central authorities for quality improvements. In order to make their future tasks easier, the enterprises may argue for lower production quotas than they think they can attain, knowing that the central planners are unable to ascertain the magnitude of such deception. The managers of enterprises will consciously engage in such behavior if their incomes and promotions are based upon attainment of the planned output levels. It is the combination of such a reward system with the information, co-ordination, and flexibility problems that can lead to energetic deception of central authorities and important violations of central decisions. Yet this reward system may be considered necessary since it provides an assurance that the planned out-put levels will be attained. Without such a guarantee, the en-tire set of national economic plans might be meaningless. Hence the attractiveness of this central-planning framework is reduced by substantial problems that lie embedded in it.

Political considerations may also affect the desirability of this planning framework. A dictatorship, in particular, may find this economic system extremely appealing since, with it, the political leaders can readily impose their will on the popu-lace. This is true, for example, in regard to the nation's savings rate. The decision to how much of the nation's produc-tion should be consumed and how much should be invested is an important factor influencing the nation's rate of economic growth. With detailed central planning, this savings rate can be raised above the level that the citizens would freely choose. The po-litical leaders may also feel that their view of the relative de-sirability of different consumption products is superior to the view of the citizens. With this planning framework, the leaders can determine the amount of each commodity that will be pro-duced. If they wish, they can ration these commodities in a detailed manner, deciding how much of each should be consumed by each citizen. Or they can permit some freedom in the con-sumer market by letting each person choose which particular commodities he will buy, given the political restriction on the total amount of each commodity that is produced. In the latter case, prices acquire an important meaning since they must be set so as to clear the market for each commodity. This price-setting task may be performed by central planners or may be left to the competitive bidding of consumers.

It is possible that a nation's political leaders, operating within this first central-planning framework, may adopt certain economic policies because they consider such policies to be necessary on the basis of their general idealogy or philosophy, even though these policies may reduce the nation's economic efficiency. Many Soviet policies, for example, have been based upon a belief in the labor theory of value, a moral repugnance toward the levying of rent or interest payments, the opinion that industrial development should have precedence over agricultural development, and a conviction that private ownership of the means of production is immoral. Detailed and comprehensive central planning may facilitate the implementation of such policies, and so this first planning framework may be preferred for ideological reasons. How can we evaluate the results of such policies? How can we measure the satisfaction received from pursuit of a morally necessary policy? Indeed, should we consider solely the satisfaction of the political leaders, or should we also consider the opinion of the populace?

There are no clear answers to the questions just posed. The questions do serve to emphasize the subjective nature of an evaluation of central planning frameworks. Because of political or philosophical considerations, the desirability of this first central planning framework varies from one nation to another, depending in each case upon the nation's kind of political system and the ideology and goals of the nation's citizens and political leaders. Similarly, for any one nation the desirability of this framework can vary over time depending upon the current political situation and philosophical beliefs.

DECENTRALIZED DECISION MAKING
WITHIN CENTRALLY DETERMINED GUIDELINES

This second framework provides for extensive decision making by enterprise personnel and local-government officials. The individual firm may play a definite role in deciding the volume and composition of its production. Enterprise personnel may have freedom to alter their production processes and to experiment with different business methods and engineering techniques. This planning framework rests upon a confidence that local initiative and local knowledge can create major improvements in the quality of commodities, can reduce production costs, and increase production volumes. To realize such achievements it is simply necessary to release the local initiative and knowledge that have been suppressed by the first planning framework. The linkages between a supplier and a customer are shortened since they need no longer pass through the

central planners' office buildings; and the linkages are improved
because direct confrontation enables enterprises to understand
the detailed needs of each, the current problems of each, and
the likelihood that another enterprise's production plans will
be disrupted. An enterprise may have freedom to negotiate
with its suppliers, so that it will obtain the quality of machinery
and equipment, raw materials, and semiprocessed goods most
appropriate for its various production processes. It is expected
that local personnel can better judge their needs for each type
of inventory than can central planners, and so increasing the
authority of local personnel will improve the smoothness with
which the firm operates. Local personnel can adapt more
rapidly to changing or unpredicted features of their business
environment than can central planners. In this manner, the
second planning framework may overcome the three basic problems of information, coordination, and flexibility that plague
the first central-planning framework.

Central planners may still exert a pervasive influence on
economic activities. Taxation, subsidies, and pricing policies
can become powerful mechanisms for intervention by the planners. For example, the planners can still affect the nation's
savings rate and can still affect the amount of each commodity
that will be produced. A dictatorship may be able to impose
its will in these spheres, and hence this second framework
might have the same sort of political appeal as the first framework. By means of taxation, planners can reduce the incomes
earned by consumers, and in this way they can reduce the
amount that the populace spends on consumption goods. The
savings rate can be raised above the level that citizens would
freely choose. The political leaders may feel that their view
of the relative desirability of different commodities is superior
to the view of the citizens. The leaders can provide different
rates of subsidies to different industries and impose different
rates of taxation in order that each industry will produce the
amount desired by the leaders. In this manner, they can affect
the total amount produced by an industry while granting, to
each individual firm or consumer, freedom in regard to production and consumption decisions.

Suppose, as in Figure 1, that the amount demanded by
customers is a function of the price charged, that the cost of
producing an additional unit of the commodity is a function of
the total amount produced, and that enterprises are seeking to
maximize their profits. The only price that will clear the
market of the commodity--without leaving customers or producers desirous of changing the amount they purchase or

FIGURE 1

Use of a Tax or Subsidy to Affect
the Quantity Produced

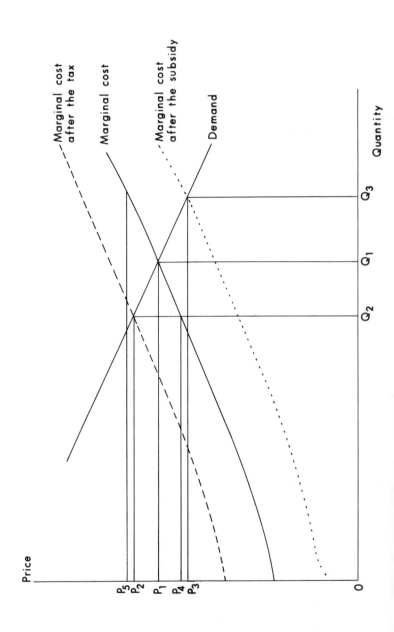

108

produce--is the price P_1. This price is the competitive equilibrium price that will tend to be established if central planners
do not intervene. The amount that will be produced and sold
at this price, during a specified time period, is represented
by Q_1 in Figure 1. The price P_1 will be optimal from the
point of view of customer welfare as seen through the eyes of
individual customers. Customers will not be willing to pay
the extra cost entailed in producing more than Q_1 of the commodity. If any amount less than Q_1 is produced, customers
will be willing to pay the cost of expanding output to Q_1.

Political leaders may disagree with this evaluation of the
relative desirability of the commodity. They may feel that
use of the relevant commodity should be restricted to the
amount Q_2. By imposing a tax--equal to the difference between
P_2 and P_4--on each unit produced, they will cause the market
price to rise to P_2, and they will cause the amount produced
and purchased to fall to Q_2. On the other hand, they can expand use of the commodity to any amount, say Q_3, by providing
a subsidy--equal to the difference between P_5 and P_3--such
that the market price will fall to P_3.

Central planners might attempt to achieve these objectives
by setting market prices directly and omitting the taxation and
subsidies discussed above. In the case of restricting use of
the commodity to Q_2, they might simply declare that P_2 should
be the market price. If producers were seeking to maximize
their profits, however, they would be willing to expand their
production and accept prices less than P_2 on a black-market
basis. Detailed supervision would be necessary to prevent
such behavior. If the market price were set at P_4, suppliers
would restrict production to Q_2. However, the excess customer
demand would require either some random rationing process
in which there could be no assurance that the customers most
desirous of the commodity would actually receive it, or else
the detailed type of rationing of the first central-planning
framework. To expand production of the commodity to Q_3,
central planners might set the market price at P_5. Customers,
however, would not purchase all that was produced at this price,
and surplus inventories would accumulate. If the price were
set at P_3, customers would demand Q_3, but suppliers would
be reluctant to expand production to the desired level. Im-
position of a legal requirement to sell to all customers who
wished to buy at the price P_3 would not solve this problem if
the average cost of production were higher than P_3 or if suppliers could shift their enterprises into the production of more
profitable commodities. In view of such difficulties, central

planners may supplement their price setting policies with
complex schemes of taxation and subsidies where rates vary
from one industry to another.

Government intervention with policies for pricing, taxation, and subsidies may be desired for ideological reasons.
Political leaders may feel that the citizens underrate the
harmful effects of some commodities, like alcoholic beverages,
and so they may implement policies to restrict consumption
of such items. On the other hand, the political leaders may
feel that citizens underrate the beneficial effects of some
things such as education, and so they may desire to expand
such activities beyond the level that free choice by the citizens
would maintain. Hence, the desirability of this planning
framework partly depends upon the degree to which the wishes
of political leaders diverge from those of the citizens.

Government intervention of this type may be desired for
reasons relating to externalities. The marginal costs depicted
in Figure 1, and on the basis of which enterprises make their
decisions, relate to <u>private costs</u> rather than <u>social costs.</u>
Political leaders may wish to restrict an industry that has a
detrimental effect on other industries or on human beings--
that is, an industry whose social costs exceed its private
costs. This may be the case with industries that pollute the
environment, for example. On the other hand, political leaders
may wish to expand an industry whose private costs exceed its
social costs, or whose social benefits exceed the price that
customers pay for the product. The profitability of an enterprise depends upon the difference between the income it receives for its products and the production costs it incurs.
This private profitability is the enterprise's guide in decision
making. From the society's point of view, the relevant measure of benefits should not be the market price of the product
but rather the integral under the demand curve. It is the demand curve that reflects the productivity or benefit of different
amounts of the commodity for potential customers. Hence
the social profitability or the difference between the integral
under the demand curve and the production costs should be
the guide in decision making, rather than the difference between the integral under the market-price line and the production costs. That is, an evaluation of consumers' surplus
should be included in production and investment decisions.
Some industries may stimulate the economic development of
other industries to an extent not reflected in the market price
or even in the demand curve for the former's products. This
is an additional reason why decisions made on the basis of

current profitability as seen through the eyes of the individual enterprise may not result in a satisfactory rate of expansion from the view of the economy as a whole. A more rapid growth of transportation and communication networks or of basic industries like steel or chemicals may increase the profitability of other economic activities. The size of such a catalytic impact varies from one industry to another, and so central planners may decide to give special encouragement to specific industries.

The form of such special encouragement may vary. The price policies, taxes, and subsidies discussed above suffer from the disadvantage that the total size of government penalties or assistance depends upon the current volume of production, which may vary considerably from year to year. The government may prefer penalties or subsidies that have a more definite ceiling. It may base them, for this reason, on the amount of capital investment. Variations in depreciation allowances or monetary grants equal to a specified percentage of the capital investment may be useful within this planning framework.

The government may wish to stimulate economically backward regions of the nation. On the basis of the profitability criterion of individual enterprises, expansion in such regions may not be undertaken. Yet, because of externalities like those mentioned above, the government may believe that investment should be encouraged. Hence central planners may offer special assistance to all enterprises that locate there -- through the guarantee of higher prices than exist elsewhere, subsidies that depend upon production volume, provision for accelerated depreciation, or grants that depend upon the size of the investment. If the government is particularly concerned about employment rates in such regions, it may base its assistance on the total wages or on the number of employees of the enterprise.

When using the type of policies discussed above, central planners face a set of problems quite different from those of the first planning framework. Prediction or forecasting acquires a new significance when enterprise personnel, local-government officials, and individual citizens have freedom to make decisions. The central planners must predict what the decentralized decisions will be. This prediction need not deal with each decision maker separately; rather it is concerned with the total result of each type of decision. When central planners wish to affect the amount of a commodity that is produced and consumed, they must alter the current set of market

prices. In considering how much the prices should be changed,
they do not need to know how much of the commodity will be
supplied by each individual producer, given a possible set of
prices, but they must predict the total amount that all producers
will supply. They do not need to know how much each individual
customer will purchase, given each possible set of prices,
but they must predict the total amount that all customers will
purchase. That is, for each commodity, central planners
must predict the industry's marginal cost or supply function
and the customers' demand function. Such prediction requires
that central planners obtain and analyze information concerning each industry or commodity. When considering policies
for regional development, they must obtain and analyze information concerning the different regions in the nation. Hence
the type of information required for the setting of centrally
determined guidelines differs considerably from the information required in the first planning framework. Here the necessary information concerns an industry, a commodity, or a
region rather than individual enterprises and citizens.

A new element of uncertainty enters in that the decentralized decision makers are under no legal obligation to behave
in precisely the way that central planners have predicted.
Central planners may survey the intentions of decentralized
decision makers, but the planners must guess the extent to
which actual behavior will resemble the surveyed intentions.
To deal with the problems involved in forecasting or prediction,
central planners must develop techniques of analysis not
needed in the first planning framework. It is possible that the
development of economic theory can also assist in dealing with
such problems. Relatively little has been written concerning
behavior patterns of decentralized decision makers operating
within centrally determined guidelines. During the past decade,
interest in this subject has increased, and a number of economists have turned their attention to an analysis of the implications of certain aspects of this planning framework. Relevant
articles include those by Arrow and Hurwicz,[2] Baumol and
Fabian,[3] Charnes, Clower, and Kortanek,[4] Domar,[5] and
Shubik.[6] It is my belief that this type of central planning is
becoming increasingly prevalent in both Russia and the West,
and that further development of pertinent economic theory is
extremely important. The remaining chapters of this book
explore several facets of this second planning framework.

For each commodity, it is likely that both the marginal
cost or supply function of a producing industry and the demand
function of its customers will change as time passes. The

market prices that central planners should set to achieve their
goals will shift as such changes occur, and some lag will occur
before the planners ascertain what the new set of relevant
prices should be. Central planners may find it quite difficult
to acquire detailed information concerning the cost and quality
changes of potential innovations, and hence the implications
of price adjustment lags are particularly germane in the realm
of technological change. Will potential cost and quality innovations actually be implemented if central planners fail to adjust
prices appropriately? Current Russian incentive schemes
base managerial bonuses on both the profit and the sales of an
enterprise. Hence, in Chapter 6, I shall discuss the implications of price lags in two different situations: when managers
behave so as to maximize their enterprises' profits and then
when they behave so as to maximize their enterprises' sales.

The manager of a small firm may be doing a better job
than the manager of a large firm even though the latter has a
greater total profit. Should bonuses and promotions be based
upon total profits or should they be based upon some other aspect of profit, such as profit per unit of capital, profit per
unit of labor, profit per unit of revenue, or profit per unit of
total production costs? The manner in which each of these
alternative maximization criteria can lead to distortions in
the enterprise's production processes is indicated in Chapter
7.

With the centralized determination of prices, local decisions concerning product quality may acquire several significant new characteristics. Monopolistic or oligopolistic behavior may appear, for example. Separate firms may collude
to reduce product quality in a manner that resembles the price
collusion of Western enterprises. Once again central planners
face a set of problems (and require techniques to solve them)
that they did not encounter in the first planning framework.
The use of differential pricing provides higher prices for high-
cost producers than it does for low-cost producers in the expectation that an expansion on the part of the high-cost producers
will result in a future decrease in their expenses. Several
aspects of pricing policies in this second planning framework
are considered in Chapter 8.

AGGREGATE ECONOMIC POLICIES WITH
DECENTRALIZED DECISION MAKING AND
WITH PRICES COMPETITIVELY DETERMINED
IN THE MARKET

With this third planning framework, central planners avoid
the problems they would encounter with either the first or
second planning frameworks.   They do not need to obtain and
analyze information concerning the production processes of
each economic enterprise, for they do not have to make decisions concerning the detailed behavior of individual firms
or citizens.   Hence they avoid the information, coordination,
and flexibility problems of the first planning framework.   They
do not need to obtain and analyze information concerning each
industry, commodity, or region since they do not institute
separate policies for each group of economic activities.   They
do not have to ascertain the proper prices, taxes, or subsidies
for each commodity or region, as they would have to do in the
second planning framework.   Rather they utilize the knowledge
and effort of all who participate in a market whenever they
participate in the market.   Each supplier and each customer
affects the configuration of prices through his bidding in the
market.   The difficulties involved in centralized price setting
are obviated by this third planning framework.   Customers may
alter the price they are willing to pay for a commodity, depending on the degree to which the supplier has succeeded in improving the quality of that commodity.   With the second planning framework, lags could occur between the time that a
potential innovation, in regard to quality or costs, is discovered
and the time that central planners change market prices in
response to the innovation.   It may be expected that such lags
will diminish when supplier and customer are free to negotiate
prices directly.   The decentralized price setting will respond
more rapidly with its rewards of higher prices for better
quality than could centralized price setting.   On the one hand,
the work of central planners is made easier when they do not
have to sift through masses of details.   On the other hand, the
entire economy may advance more rapidly because the prices,
upon which suppliers and customers base their decisions, reflect relative needs and scarcities more accurately than they
could when set by central planners.
     With this third framework, central planners are concerned
with aggregate data.   They wish to maintain full employment
in the economy, and they may seek to achieve this through

fiscal and monetary policies. If a depression threatens, they
may increase government expenditures, reduce tax rates, and
expand the money supply, thereby increasing aggregate demand.
They may wish to restrain any inflationary situation by reducing
aggregate demand through increases in tax rates, a diminution
of government expenditures, and a reduction in the money supply. They may even manipulate tariff rates to avoid a depression or to restrain inflation. Tariff policy may be used to
foster a broad development of industrial activity in the nation
or to protect the agricultural sector from foreign competition.
Such policies are not aimed at specific enterprises or even at
specific industries, regions, or commodities. All enterprises
and citizens face the same set of rates in regard to taxation,
interest payments, and tariffs.
      The problems encountered in this planning framework have
been discussed at length by critics of Western capitalism.
Central planners experience a forecasting or prediction problem
in deciding upon the degree to which they should alter existing
tax rates, government expenditures, and money supply. They
must not only predict what would happen without any such
changes; they must also predict the economy's reaction to each
of the possible alterations they might make. The difficulties
involved in such forecasting and the possibility of errors in
this prediction process may mean that an economic depression
or an inflation could, in fact, develop.
      A firm may become a monopolist in the provision of a
certain commodity, and it may be able to raise the price of
the commodity not because of improvements in quality, but
rather because the firm possesses market power. A number
of separate firms may enter explicit or tacit agreements in
order to achieve price increases without quality improvements.
The existence of oligopolies and monopolistic competitors may
distort market processes such that income distribution is un-
fairly affected and customers' purchases are less than would
be optimal. On the other hand, customers may possess monopolistic power such that they force a decrease in the price they
pay for a commodity below the price they would have to pay in
a competitive market.
      External economies may be disregarded, so that an in-
dustry receives less investment than it should. External diseconomies may be ignored, such that one industry exerts a
harmful impact on other economic activities or on individual
citizens. Hence the nation's rate of economic growth may be
retarded and its environment may become polluted. Uniform
monetary and fiscal policies may not affect all industries or

all geographic regions or all socioeconomic classes equally.
A policy of tight money, increased taxation rates, and reductions in government expenditures may be implemented to restrain national inflation, yet its effects may be concentrated
in low-income groups, depressed economic regions, city
slums, and the housing sector. National policies to stimulate
growth may be unable to affect the pockets of poverty that have
persisted in many of the economically advanced Western nations.
From this discussion, we can see that a variety of significant
weaknesses or shortcomings may permeate this third central
planning framework.

THE TRANSITION

Several important comments can be made concerning the
shift of a nation from one central-planning framework to
another. Each framework requires the collection and analysis
of a different type of information. Within each framework,
central planners use a different set of techniques for intervention in economic activities, and they encounter a different set
of problems as they perform their tasks. Hence a movement
from one framework to another is a major undertaking. It requires that central planners be retrained to fulfill their new
roles. Such retraining must be achieved by means of direct
experience with the new types of information and techniques
that suddenly become relevant. It might be expected that the
need to accumulate experience in the new roles would make
the first few years of the transition most difficult. The nation
would endure an initial period of disappointment with the new
framework, followed by an increasing degree of satisfaction
as time passed. It might also be expected that the central
planners and political leaders would fully appreciate the problems of the new framework only after they encountered these
problems directly. Hence the transition from one framework
to another might be marked by both advances and retreats as
the relative advantages and disadvantages of the new framework became more apparent.

As time passes, the relative advantages and disadvantages
of each planning framework will change. Improvements will
be made in the various methods of collecting and analyzing
data, and these improvements may be expected to reduce the
shortcomings of certain planning techniques. A revolution in
computer technology, for example, may increase the appeal

of the first framework of detailed central planning. Changes
in a nation's political attitudes may also alter the relative desirability of the planning frameworks. A nation may be more
likely to shift from the first to the second framework if its
leaders decide to ignore ideological antipathy towards interest,
rent, or profit. In all three frameworks, political leaders can
affect the nation's savings rate, yet the confidence they can
feel in this regard varies from the certainty of detailed central
planning to the forecasts of the second and third planning frameworks. Although both the first and second frameworks enable
planners to effect the quantities produced of each commodity,
the degree of certainty concerning the actual outcomes may
vary considerably. In view of these aspects, political leaders
may change their advocacy of a particular framework as their
attitude towards risk and uncertainty shifts.

The importance of external economies, external diseconomies, and imperfections in the market varies from one industry, commodity, or region to another. Recognizing this fact,
a nation may find it desirable to shift to a new planning framework in dealing with some economic activities, but retain its
current planning framework in dealing with others. A nation
that operates within the third planning framework, for example,
may choose to have its government own and operate some
specific enterprises in the direct fashion of the first planning
framework. Such a nation may also decide to involve its
central planners in price setting within certain markets. In
view of this, it is appropriate to think of a spectrum of central
planning frameworks and to consider the three frameworks discussed above as illustrative simplifications rather than as accurate descriptions of existing institutional structures.

NOTES

1.   J. M. Montias, Central Planning in Poland, (New
Haven: Yale University Press, 1962), p. 107.

2.   K. J. Arrow and L. Hurwicz, "Decentralization and
Computation in Resource Allocation," Essays in Economics
and Econometrics, (Chapel Hill: University of North Carolina,
1960), pp. 34-104.

3.   W. J. Baumol and R. Fabian, "Decomposition, Pricing
for Decentralization and External Economics," Management
Science, XI, 1 (September, 1964).

4.   A. Charnes, R. W. Clower, and K. O. Kortanek, "Effective Control Through Coherent Decentralization with Preemptive Goals," Econometrica, XXXV, 2, (April, 1967), 294-320.

5.   E. D. Domar, "The Societ Collective Farm As a Producer Cooperative," American Economic Review, LVI, 4 (September, 1966), 734-757.

6.   M. Shubik, "Incentives, Decentralized Control, the Assignment of Joint Costs and Internal Pricing" (Cowles Foundation Paper, no. 178, Yale University, 1962).

CHAPTER **6** PROFIT OR SALES
MAXIMIZATION AND THE
EFFECTS OF LAGS IN
CENTRALLY DETERMINED
PRICES

For each commodity in the economy, both the marginal
cost or supply function of the producing industry and the demand function of its customers will change as time passes.
If central planners, operating within the second planning
framework, set market prices so as to achieve specific goals,
then it is likely that a revision of market prices will be necessary whenever supply or demand conditions change. A lag
may occur between the time that price shifts should be made
and the time that central planners actually achieve these
price modifications. Central planners must first ascertain
that such price shifts are necessary, then they must decide
what specific tax, subsidy, or regulation should be improved;
and finally both suppliers and customers must react to the new
government policies. Errors in the forecasts or judgment of
central planners may prolong such time lags. Central planners
may find it particularly difficult to obtain detailed information
concerning the cost and quality changes that potential innovations would entail if implemented; and so the implications of
time lags in the price adjustment process are especially important in the realm of technological change. At the present
time, the incentive schemes used in the Russian enterprises
operating under this planning system include bonuses based
on both profit maximization and sales maximization. In view
of this, it appears useful to consider the implications of time
lags when an enterprise operates so as to maximize its profits and also when it operates so as to maximize its sales.
As we have seen in the first part of this book, enterprises
operating under the detailed Stalin-Khrushchev type of central planning were criticized for failing to produce the desired assortment of products, for not being sufficiently
interested in cost-reducing innovations, and for not being
sufficiently concerned about improving the quality of their

products. This chapter focuses its attention on the question whether such shortcomings are likely to reappear in the second planning framework if lags occur in the process of central price setting.

Throughout this chapter it is assumed that, for any commodity, marginal and average costs rise as the total amount produced increases within the range of quantities being considered. This assumption rests on the belief that different firms experience different production costs and that low-cost suppliers either are limited in their expansion possibilities by physical or financial constraints or else encounter rising expenses as they do expand their production. In Figure 2, the industry's marginal and averages costs are depicted as being U-shaped, the form traditionally assumed in Western economic analysis, although the only aspect of these curves necessary for the following arguments is that they rise as the amount produced increases in the range of quantities being considered. Individual enterprises may produce several commodities. Our examination considers each commodity separately, concentrating on the minimum additional cost the nation must incur to produce more of the commodity, the average cost it experiences in producing different amounts of the commodity, and the prices that it is willing to pay to obtain various amounts of the commodity. It is assumed in this chapter that the demand schedules are the ideal or socially approved schedules. It may be that the commodity being considered is a consumption good and that the demand schedules reflect the market demands of individual consumers. In this case, it is assumed that consumers have been taxed to achieve the income distribution that central authorities desire. Whether the commodity is a consumption good or an item necessary in another industry's production process, it is assumed that the demand and cost curves are the schedules that exist after central planners have imposed a tax on the commodity or have provided a subsidy. The original market price, in each case, is the price that central planners consider socially optimal prior to any shifts or potential shifts in these schedules.

AN AUTONOMOUS SHIFT IN DEMAND

In Figure 2, suppose that average and marginal cost for the industry are represented by MC_1 and AC_1, respectively and that demand for the product is responsive to price in the

FIGURE 2

The Implications of Changes in an
Industry's Cost and Demand Functions

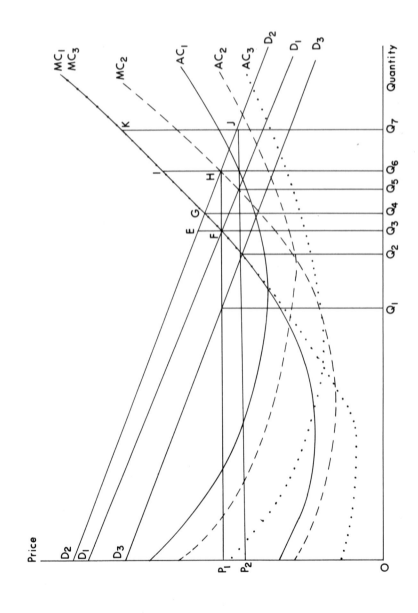

manner represented by D_1D_1. Price and output are at the optimal levels P_1 and Q_3, respectively. Suppose that an autonomous shift in demand occurs from D_1D_1 to D_2D_2. If producers are maximizing sales they will expand output to Q_6; if they are maximizing profits they will continue to produce Q_3, as long as a black market is prevented. Neither output level is equal to the optimal amount Q_4.

Under the sales-maximization criterion, the cost to society of producing the excess amount Q_6-Q_4 is represented in Figure A by $\int_{Q_4}^{Q_6} MC_1$. The amount that customers are willing to pay for the extra Q_6-Q_4 is represented by $\int_{Q_4}^{Q_6} D_2D_2$. Clearly, the former exceeds the latter and the difference or the area GHI represents the loss to society from producing Q_6 instead of Q_4. Under profit maximization, the customers would be willing to pay $\int_{Q_3}^{Q_4} D_2D_2$ for the amount Q_4-Q_3. The cost to the economy of producing Q_4-Q_3 would be $\int_{Q_3}^{Q_4} MC_1$, and the loss to society due to underproduction can be represented by the area EFG. It is not clear which of GHI or EFG is greater--and hence it is not clear which criterion will result in the greater misallocation of resources.

Suppose that an autonomous shift in demand from D_1D_1 to D_3D_3 occurs. Both profit-maximizing and sales-maximizing firms will tend to reduce output to Q_1 if they must continue to sell their product at the price P_1. Excess supply will exist in the market until they do reach Q_1. Excess supply can exist even though total output of the particular product is less than the optimal amount Q_2.

INNOVATION THAT REDUCES BOTH AVERAGE AND MARGINAL COST WITHOUT AFFECTING THE DEMAND FOR THE PRODUCT

Suppose that a suggested change in technology can reduce both average and marginal costs for an industry from AC_1 to AC_2 and from MC_1 to MC_2 respectively in Figure 2. The demand for the product is represented by D_1D_1. Maximization of social welfare will require expansion of industrial production from Q_3 to Q_5.

Under profit maximization, if no collusion exists each firm will adopt the innovation and will expand its production. Total industrial production will tend towards Q_6, exceeding Q_5; and excess supply of the product may well exist. This tendency towards sectoral overproduction will continue until central planners do lower the product price to P_2. The sales-maximizing industry, on the other hand, will not be interested in the innovation since its ability to expand output and sales would not be improved. Hence it might tend to produce less than the optimal amount Q_5 and its average cost might well be higher than that in a profit-maximizing industry.

INNOVATION THAT REDUCES AVERAGE COST BUT RAISES MARGINAL COST IN THE RELEVANT OUTPUT RANGE WITHOUT AFFECTING THE DEMAND FOR THE PRODUCT

Suppose that the demand for a product is represented by D_2D_2 in Figure 2; average and marginal cost are represented by AC_2 and MC_2 respectively. Price has been set at P_1 and output equals Q_6. It is at least theoretically possible that an innovation could reduce average cost from AC_2 to AC_3 and at the same time shift marginal cost from MC_2 to MC_3, where MC_3 is congruent with MC_1 for large quantities of the commodity but lies below both MC_1 and MC_2 for small quantities.

For maximization of social welfare, the industry should adopt the new technology if AC_2Q_6 minus AC_3Q_4 (where AC_2 is calculated at output Q_6 and AC_3 at output Q_4) exceeds $\int_{Q_4}^{Q_6} D_2D_2$. Hence whether or not the new technology should be adopted depends on the precise nature of the demand and cost curves. The sales-maximizing industry will disregard such an innovation regardless of the precise nature of demand and cost curves. The profit-maximizing industry will adopt it if AC_2Q_6 minus AC_3Q_3 (where AC_2 is calculated at output Q_6 and AC_3 at output Q_3) exceeds $P_1(Q_3-Q_6)$. This decision-making rule is not the rule for maximization of social welfare, and it is possible that the innovation will be adopted when it should be ignored. Even if the profit-maximizing industry should innovate and does so, nevertheless, its output of Q_3 will be less than the socially optimal amount Q_4, and excess demand will exist for this product.

INNOVATION THAT IMPROVES THE QUALITY OF THE PRODUCT, INCREASING DEMAND BUT RAISING BOTH AVERAGE AND MARGINAL COST

Suppose that demand is represented by D_1D_1 and average and marginal costs are represented by AC_2 and MC_2, respectively. The product price is set at P_2 and output equals Q_5. Suppose that a quality improvement can shift the demand for the product from D_1D_1 to D_2D_2 but that this quality improvement will raise both average and marginal cost from AC_2 to AC_1 and MC_2 to MC_1 respectively.

It is clear that the profit-maximizing industry will not be interested in adopting the innovation unless the product's price is increased. That is, any such innovation definitely requires prior consultation with the central planners. Sales-maximizing firms will be quick to adopt the innovation since it will permit them to expand sales from Q_5 to Q_7. Clearly, this expansion is too great from the view of maximizing social welfare. In order to determine which position is worse, it is necessary to compare the amounts:

$$\int_0^{Q_4} D_2D_2 - \int_0^{Q_4} MC_1 = \int_0^{Q_7} D_2D_2 + \int_0^{Q_7} MC_1.$$

and

$$\int_0^{Q_4} D_2D_2 - \int_0^{Q_4} MC_1 - \int_0^{Q_5} D_1D_1 + \int_0^{Q_5} MC_2.$$

It is possible that the innovation can not improve social welfare even if the optimal amount Q_4 is produced; that is

$$\int_0^{Q_4} D_2D_2 - \int_0^{Q_4} MC_1 \text{ may be less than } \int_0^{Q_5} D_1D_1 - \int_0^{Q_5} MC_2$$

INNOVATION THAT IMPROVES THE QUALITY OF THE PRODUCT, INCREASING DEMAND, RAISING AVERAGE COST, AND REDUCING MARGINAL COST IN THE RELEVANT OUTPUT RANGE

Suppose that demand is represented by D_1D_1; average and marginal cost are represented by AC_3 and MC_3 respectively.

Price is set at P_1 and output is Q_3. Suppose that an innovation can shift demand from D_1D_1 to D_2D_2, but it raises average cost from AC_3 to AC_2 and shifts marginal cost from MC_3 to MC_2.

In this case, the profit-miximizing industry might adopt the new technology. It would do so if $(P_1-AC_2)Q_6$ exceeds $(P_1-AC_3)Q_3$, where AC_2 is calculated at Q_6 and AC_3 at Q_3. It is impossible to say a priori whether its output Q_6 would be greater or less than the optimal output should it adopt the innovation since MC_2 might intersect D_2D_2 to the left or right of H. It is clear that this decision-making rule varies from the socially optimal rule that such an innovation should be im-plemented if $\int_0^{Q_6} D_2D_2 - AC_2Q_6$ exceeds $\int_0^{Q_3} D_1D_1 - AC_3Q_3.$

Sales-maximizing firms would be quick to adopt the new technology, whether or not the latter criterion were met.

An important conclusion of this analysis is that, with either profit or sales maximization, the extent to which price adjustment lags will deter the adoption of innovations depends upon the type of innovation being considered; and with profit maximization it also depends upon the precise shapes of the demand and cost curves. Even if innovations are adopted, production may not occur at the optimal level. In several cases, it is impossible to ascertain a priori whether misallocation of resources will be greater with profit maximization or with sales maximization. The sales-maximization criterion seems especially unsatisfactory in regard to the adoption of cost-reducing innovations and with respect to its tendency to result in excess supply of the commodity. The profit-maximization criterion seems especially unsatisfactory in regard to the adoption of quality-improving innovations and with respect to its tendency to result in excess demand for the commodity. The relative disadvantages of the sales-maximization criterion may be more obvious to the populace than the relative disadvantages of the profit-maximization criterion. Everyone may notice the production of excess supplies of a commodity, whereas no one may notice the sectoral under-production of the profit criterion. This underproduction may not always result in unsatisfied demand at the given product price; queues, for example, would not be formed to obtain the commodity. Here we may see a political reason for lead-ers to choose profit rather than sales maximization as a central criterion for purchase and production decisions at the enterprise level.

CHAPTER 7 ALTERNATIVE PROFIT-
MAXIMIZATION CRITERIA

The provision of bonuses and the award of promotions on
the basis of an enterprise's total profits is not an entirely satisfactory approach even if central planners have managed to
set prices in the desired pattern. The criterion of total profits
may be both morally inequitable and also economically disadvantageous if the manager of a small firm is doing a better job
than the manager of a large firm. The manager of a small firm
may deserve a larger bonus and more rapid promotion than
the manager of the large firm even though the latter may be
earning a larger total profit. If the small firm is free to expand as quickly as it wishes, then it may borrow additional
capital, hire extra employees, and become a large firm itself.
Institutional barriers may prevent such expansion, however.
The small firm may not be able to borrow as much capital or
hire as many employees as it wishes. The banking system, for
example, may place ceilings upon the amount of credit it will
extend to a small firm, basing such restrictions on some specified debt/equity ratio. The commodity market within which
the small firm operates may be limited in scope and the firm
may have to diversify its production activities in order to expand. Such diversification may entail a considerable passage
of time. During the time interval required for expansion and
diversification, the manager of the small firm shoulders a
lesser responsibility than he is qualified to bear. The economy's success is diminished by such a situation and the manager
may justifiably feel that his monetary rewards have been too low.
    Russian economists and political leaders have noted these
limitations of the total profits criterion and have suggested a
number of alternative maximization criteria. The following

The material in this chapter was summarized in the author's
article, "A Note on Soviet Profit Maximization," The Canadian
Journal of Economics, II, 3, August, 1969.

four criteria have each received considerable attention: (1) profit per unit of labor; (2) profit per unit of capital; (3) the ratio of profit to total production costs; (4) the ratio of profit to total revenue. Yet each of these may lead to distortions in production processes that reduce the nation's total production below the level it could otherwise attain. There are various approaches one could use to illustrate the distortions caused by these alternative criteria. Much of this chapter employs elementary calculus for this purpose. The advantage of this approach is that it can be applied to each of the four alternative criteria. As indicated below, when a firm is instructed to maximize its total profits it will extend the use of each of its supplies or inputs until the marginal-revenue product of the input is equal to the price that the firm must pay for the input. If each firm operates on this basis, then the marginal-revenue product of each particular input will be the same in every firm; and no reallocation of inputs among firms could increase total production. The achievement of this optimal situation is the result of each firm simply maximizing its total profits. When a firm is instructed to maximize some other aspect of profit, however, it will not extend the use of each of its inputs until the marginal revenue product of the input is equal to the price that the firm must pay for the input. If each firm operates on this basis, there is no longer any reason for believing that the marginal-revenue product of each particular input will be the same in every firm. Hence, the situation that results may not be optimal in that some reallocation of inputs among firms might serve to increase the nation's total production. This analysis assumes that no individual firm can change the market prices of the inputs it buys or of the commodities it sells merely by varying the amounts of them that it buys and sells. That is, each firm makes its decisions on the basis of the prices that are given to it in the market. No firm makes decisions in the expectation that it can alter those prices.

   The distortion of certain enterprise decisions as a result of each of the profit maximization criteria mentioned above can be readily perceived with the use of the following notation: Π = total profits; Q = units produced of the particular commodity; X_i = units used of input i ; P_Q = price per unit of Q; P_i = price per unit of input i . The case of maximization of total profit is treated first. Maximization of profit per unit of capital can be treated with the same calculations as can maximization of profit per unit of labor; so these alternative criteria, labelled (a) and (b), are not distinguished in the calculus that follows.

$$\Pi = P_Q Q - \sum_{i=1}^{n} P_i X_i.$$

The firm maximizing total profits increases use of each input, X_i ($i = 1, 2, \ldots, n$) until, for that input,

$$\partial \Pi / \partial X_i = \partial (P_Q Q) / \partial X_i - P_i = 0$$

i.e., until

$$\partial (P_Q Q) / \partial X_i = P_i.$$

(a) and (b). The firm maximizing profits per unit of one of the inputs, X_j, increases use of that input until

$$\frac{\partial \left(\dfrac{\Pi}{X_j} \right)}{\partial X_j} = \frac{X_j \left(\dfrac{\partial P_Q Q}{\partial X_j} \right) - P_Q Q}{X_j^2} + \frac{\displaystyle\sum_{\substack{i=1 \\ i \neq j}}^{n} P_i X_i}{X_j^2} = 0$$

i.e., until

$$\frac{\partial (P_Q Q)}{\partial X_j} = \frac{P_Q Q - \displaystyle\sum_{\substack{i=1 \\ i \neq j}}^{n} P_i X_i}{X_j} = \frac{\Pi + P_j X_j + \displaystyle\sum_{\substack{i=1 \\ i \neq 1}}^{n} P_i X_i - \displaystyle\sum_{\substack{i=1 \\ i \neq i}}^{n} P_i X_i}{X_j} = \frac{\Pi}{X_j} +$$

And this firm increases use of X_i ($i \neq j$) until

$$\partial (P_Q Q) / \partial X_i = P_i.$$

(c) The firm maximizing the ratio of profit to total productions costs increases use of each input X_j, until

$$\frac{\partial \left(\dfrac{\Pi}{\displaystyle\sum_{i=1}^{n} P_i X_i} \right)}{\partial X_j} = \frac{\partial \left(\dfrac{P_Q Q}{\displaystyle\sum_{i=1}^{n} P_i X_i} - 1 \right)}{\partial X_j} = \frac{\displaystyle\sum_{i=1}^{n} P_i X_i \dfrac{\partial (P_Q Q)}{\partial X_j} - P_Q Q P_j}{\left(\displaystyle\sum_{i=1}^{n} P_i X_i \right)^2} = 0$$

i.e., until

$$\frac{\partial (P_Q Q)}{\partial X_j} = \frac{P_Q Q P_j}{\displaystyle\sum_{i=1}^{n} P_i X_i} = P_j \left(\frac{\Pi + \displaystyle\sum_{i=1}^{n} P_i X_i}{\displaystyle\sum_{i=1}^{n} P_i X_i} \right).$$

(d) The firm maximizing the ratio of profit to total revenue increases use of each input X_j, until

$$\frac{\partial\left(\dfrac{\Pi}{P_Q Q}\right)}{\partial X_j} = \frac{\partial\left(1 - \dfrac{\Sigma P_i X_i}{P_Q Q}\right)}{\partial X_j} = \frac{-P_Q Q P_j + \sum\limits_{i=1}^{n} P_i X_i \dfrac{\partial(P_Q Q)}{\partial X_j}}{\left(P_Q Q\right)^2} = 0$$

i. e. , until

$$\frac{\partial(P_Q Q)}{\partial X_j} = \frac{P_Q Q P_j}{\sum\limits_{i=1}^{n} P_i X_i} = P_j \left(\frac{\Pi + \sum\limits_{i=1}^{n} P_i X_i}{\sum\limits_{i=1}^{n} P_i X_i}\right).$$

As seen above, when enterprises maximize total profits, the marginal-revenue product of labor is the same in every enterprise since in every enterprise it equals the price of labor; and the marginal revenue product of capital is the same in every enterprise since in every enterprise it equals the price of capital. In cases (a), (b), (c), and (d), however, the marginal revenue products of labor and/or capital no longer equal the prices of labor and/or capital, and they may not diverge equally from these prices in every firm. Hence the marginal revenue products of labor and/or capital need not be the same in every firm. Because of this, total production may well be less than in the case where total profits are max-imized; and, to maximize total production, labor and capital have to be reallocated until their marginal revenue products are the same in every firm. From this we can see that the precise form of the maximization criterion is of decisive im-portance for efficient production.

Several Western economists have developed theoretical analyses of a cooperative where employees are members of the cooperative and receive a share of the profit. Here it might be expected that decision makers will act so as to max-imize profits per unit of labor. Evsey Domar has discussed two such situations in his article "The Soviet Collective Farm As a Producer Cooperative."[1] In his Pure Model, Domar assumes that the cooperative can admit or expel members in an attempt to maximize the income of the members who remain. In this case, the decisions of the cooperative differ consider-ably from those of a firm maximizing its total profits. An

increase in any rent that the cooperative must pay will cause
the cooperative to expand its output. An increase in the prices
it must pay for its inputs will also lead the cooperative to expand production. An increase in the price it receives for its
output may cause the cooperative to reduce its output level;
that is, the supply curve of a cooperative may be negatively
sloped. Domar feels that, in practice, a cooperative will
not be able to admit and expel members easily once it has
been organized. Because of this belief, he presents a second
discussion in which he assumes that membership is fixed and
that the supply of labor facing the cooperative is a positive
function of the income the workers receive. In this second
case, the cooperative's behavior resembles that of the firm
maximizing total profits more closely that was true in the
first case. Here a cooperative will reduce its output when rents
are raised or when the prices of inputs are raised. The amount
of output that this cooperative will supply is a positive function
of the price it can receive for its output. Domar's second
model is no doubt more representative of Soviet collective
farms today than is his Pure Model. In regard to future reforms, the Pure Model, with its freedom to admit and expel
members, may in fact become relevant. For a nation that
has emphasized the labor theory of value, maximization of
profit per unit of labor seems an obvious criterion to use for
bonuses and promotions. With the use of this criterion in
enterprises other than cooperatives, the queer behavior of
Domar's Pure Model could become economically significant.

Current debate in the U.S.S.R. had given rise to an argument that what firms should maximize is profit per unit of
capital. Professor Liberman, a distinguished Soviet economist,
has lent his authority to this proposal with comments such as
the following:

> Discussion should focus, as I see it, not on the abso-
> lute total of profits, since the larger the enterprise,
> the greater--all other things being equal--will be
> its profits. This means that to evaluate effective-
> ness, profits must be related to some base that
> characterizes the enterprise's capacity. For such
> a base, it would be most desirable to take the value
> of the enterprise's productive capital. Then the
> evaluation will be made according to the profit-
> ability of production understood as the ratio of profits
> to the value of productive capital. [2]

This proposal can be analyzed easily in the context of
Domar's article. All that is needed is to replace Domar's
phrase "dividends per labor unit" with "profits per unit of

capital." Domar's comments are valid for both maximization
criteria. However, a firm maximizing profit per unit of
capital can perhaps admit and expel capital more easily than
a cooperative maximizing profit per unit of labor can admit
and expel labor. Hence Domar's Pure Model is more likely
to be relevant when firms maximize profits per unit of capital than when they are organized as cooperatives. In view of
this, it is more likely that the supply curve of the product will
be negatively sloped, and that an increase in rents or the prices
of inputs will result in an increase in output.

The reader may have noticed, in the calculus presented
above, that the third and fourth criteria lead to similar results. A firm maximizing the ratio of profits to total   roduc-
tion costs and a firm maximizing the ratio of profits to total
revenue increase use of each input to the same extent. In
neither case, of course, does the use of the input correspond
to the amount that would be used by a firm maximizing its
total profits, unless the firm's profit is zero. This result
can be explained by considering these criteria in the situation
depicted by Figure 3, where P_1 is the market price of the
firm's output. To maximize the ratio of total profits to total
production costs, the firm must maximize the ratio of average
profit to average cost; that is, the ratio XY/XZ. With a
constant price for its output, the firm can only achieve this
goal by producing the quantity, Q_1, at which its average cost
is minimized. To maximize the ratio of total profits to total
revenue, the firm must maximize the ratio of average profit
to average revenue; that is, the ratio XY/XZ. This the firm
can only do by producing the quantity Q_1 at which its average
cost is minimized. Hence, both these criteria lead the firm
to produce the quantity Q_1 which is less than the optimal
amount Q_2 produced by a firm maximizing its total profit. If
the level of minimum average cost differs among firms, then
it is not optimal from the nation's point of view for all firms
to minimize their average costs. Rather, it is advantageous
to eliminate certain high-cost firms and to extend the production of low-cost suppliers. The only case where the implications of cost minimization are no different from the implications of the maximization of total profits occurs when all firms
experience the same minimum average cost, when the price
is set equal to that minimum average cost, and, consequently,
when each firm receives zero profit.

In concluding this chapter, we should note that none of the
profit-maximization criteria discussed here is without shortcomings, and that it is impossible on the basis of theoretical

FIGURE 3

Output Determination of Firms Maximizing the Ratio
of Profit to Total Production Costs and
the Ratio of Profit to Total Revenue

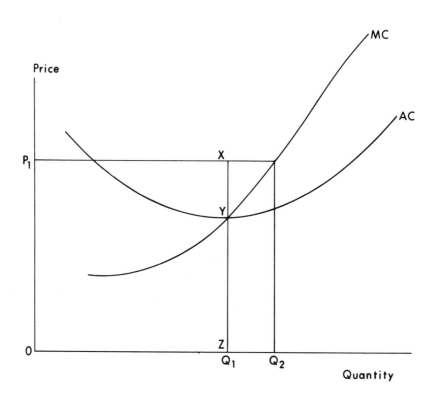

analysis alone to predict the extent or economic significance of such shortcomings should a particular criterion be applied. Which criterion is best is a question that only actual experience can answer. Hence the profit-criterion problem serves to emphasize our lack of knowledge concerning the second planning framework, and it indicates the uncertainty a nation experiences in shifting to the second framework from one of the other economic systems, about which a considerable understanding has already accumulated.

NOTES

1. E. D. Domar, "The Soviet Collective Farm as Producer Cooperative," American Economic Review (September, 1966) pp. 734-757.

2. Y. Liverman, "Once More on the Plan, Profits, and Bonuses," Pravda (September 20, 1964) p. 3 as translated in the Current Digest of the Soviet Press, XVI, 38 20-21.

CHAPTER **8** PROBLEMS OF IMPERFECT
MARKETS AND OF
DIFFERENTIAL PRICING

    Central planners engage in a price-setting process even
when they operate within the first economic framework discussed in Chapter 5--that is, even when they are responsible
for all details concerning each economic activity in the nation.
In such a situation, the central planners may impose their
wishes concerning the pattern of consumer goods to be produced.
They will also participate in decisions concerning production
volumes of the various intermediate goods like different types
of machinery and equipment. The relative weights that planners
attach to the value or usefulness of additional units of the various commodities can be considered as prices. When the
planners reach a solution in regard to the relative quantities
to be produced, they have at the same time reached a decision
concerning the relative value or usefulness of additional units;
and hence they have implicitly settled upon relative prices.
The role and importance of such prices are restricted, however. Enterprises receive precise orders pertaining to the
inputs they are to use in their production processes and the
commodities they are to produce. Any prices or relative
weights attached to inputs or outputs are not to be the basis
for enterprise decisions, since in theory, individual enterprises are not to engage in decision making.
    Under the Stalin-Khrushchev planning system, the Russian
government awarded bonuses to enterprises for fulfilment of
their production plans. The government officials realized
that the local personnel of the individual firm could affect the
volume of their firm's output. Although they worked for a
stipulated number of hours, the personnel could vary production in accordance with the effort, initiative, and thought they
applied to their tasks. Because many enterprises produced
more than one commodity, government officials required some
method of weighting the different commodities to arrive at an
index of a firm's total output. Without such weights or prices,
a change in the ratio of these different products to each other,

in quantity terms, would preclude comparisons of total output. It would be impossible, without prices, to compare one firm's production levels over time, to compare production volumes among firms, or to compare an enterprise's actual output with its total planned output. Furthermore, prices had to be adjusted in accordance with alterations in demand and supply conditions for, otherwise, the efforts of individual firms to maximize their output could result in the production of an undesirable mix of commodities.

In the past, Russian government officials have also used cost reductions as a success criterion on which to base bonuses and promotions. The government officials realized that the local personnel of the individual firm could affect the firm's production costs. Although the firm received specified amounts of each input, the local personnel could waste or abuse the supplies it received. On the other hand, the personnel could exercise diligent caution in making fullest possible use of the firm's supplies. If the firm used more than one input, the relative value to society of these different inputs would have to be clearly stated. Otherwise, neither the personnel nor the government officials could ascertain the extent to which cost had truly been reduced when the input mix per unit of output had changed.

Under the Stalin-Khrushchev planning system, the role and importance of price setting were restricted in that a firm could not change its mix of inputs or outputs significantly without the prior approval of the nation's central planners. The firm's personnel could alter the initiative, effort, and care that they applied to their jobs, but this variability of personnel productivity was the only legally recognized sphere within which prices could influence enterprise decisions. In practice, failures of supervision did extend this decision-making role of the firm. An enterprise might act contrary to the clearly expressed wishes of central planners, in the expectation that its infractions would not be detected. A firm, for example, might refuse to implement quality improving innovations if such innovations would raise its costs and, consequently, would reduce its production volume. Centrally issued declarations concerning the need for quality improvements might be ignored. To the extent that their wishes were being violated without punishment, central planners could have used prices to assist in eliciting the production responses they sought. When they could not enforce their commands for quality improvements, central planners could have raised the prices of more advanced models of the commodity. The first part of this book has indicated that both the variability of personnel productivity and the undetected infractions of centrally issued decrees affected Russia's economic activities to such an extent that the nation's leaders were extremely dissatisfied. It was not until 1965 that these leaders decided to alter prices systematically and frequently in order that the decisions of individual firms, guided by these prices, would be in accord with the wishes of central planners. Even without any expansion in the rights and responsibilities of the individual firm, a revitalized approach to price setting could have been a reasonable reform. With the new emphasis on decentralized decision making, the urgent need for a more adequate price structure has become apparent to everyone. The difficulties involved in price setting have not been as widely recognized. Serious complications may develop, for example, if a market is not perfectly competitive. If monopoly, duopoly, oligopoly, or monopolistic competition exists, it may not be sufficient for central planners to rely upon price setting: they may also have to engage in the setting of detailed quality standards. A firm operating in an imperfectly competitive market may be able to increase its profit by debasing the quality of its products. Such action may be contrary to the wishes of the central planners, and yet it cannot be prevented by price setting alone.

MONOPOLY

Suppose a monopolist is producing a commodity for which central planners have set the price P_1 in Figure 4. To produce this commodity, the monopolist experiences marginal and average costs indicated by the Curves MC_1 and AC_1 respectively. The demand for this produce is indicated by D_1D_1. It may be expected that the monopolist will produce the quantity Q_1 and earn a profit equal to P_1 minus AC_1 (at the output Q_1) times Q_1. However, the monopolist may be able to earn a greater profit by reducing the quality of his commodity, even though such a reduction will curtail the demand for his product. Suppose, for example, that the monopolist can reduce his costs from AC_1 to AC_2 and from MC_1 to MC_2, while the demand for the inferior product shifts from D_1D_1 to D_2D_2. The monopolist's profit is now equal to P_1 minus AC_2 (at the output Q_2) times Q_2. It may be that this profit from the interior product exceeds the profit the monopolist could earn on his original quality of the commodity.

FIGURE 4

Monopoly and the Determination of Quality
with Central Price Setting

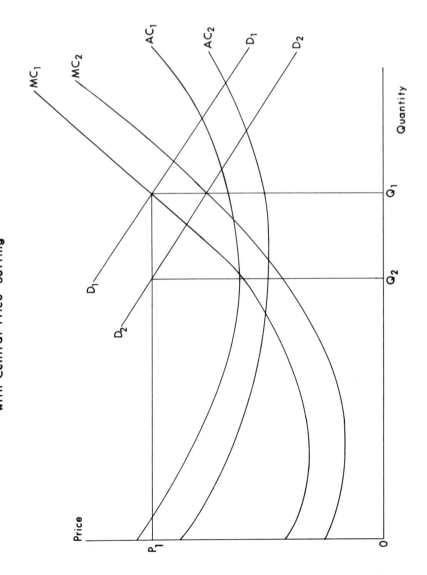

FIGURE 5

The Effect of Quality Variations
on a Monopolist's Profit

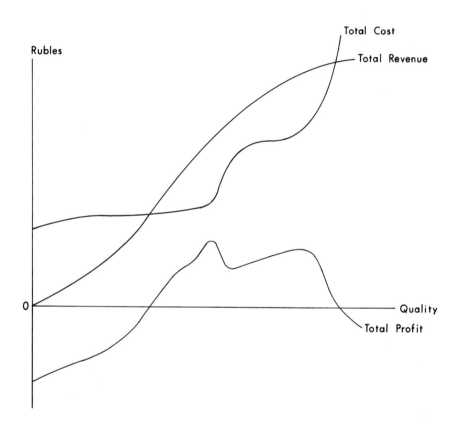

The monopolist may have no way of ascertaining the precise extent to which the demand for his product will shift with
a reduction in quality. He may have to experiment with such
quality variations. It should be noted that even if the product
were subject to gradual reductions in quality, nevertheless,
it is not clear that quality reductions would affect the monopolist's profit in a consistent manner. As the monopolist decreased the product quality, he might encounter alternating
stretches of increasing and decreasing profit.

Suppose that quality can be measured in ordinal fashion.
As indicated in Figure 5, the monopolist may earn a different
total revenue for each type of product quality. The higher
the quality of the product, the more total revenue the monopolist will earn. Since the price of the product has been set by
central planners, there may be some quality level at which no
customers are willing to pay the required price for the product.
Let this quality level be represented by the intersection of the
quality axis with the axis on which rubles are measured. At
this quality level, total revenue will be zero. As the quality
of the product is improved, the monopolist's total costs rise.
Even to produce a quality of product that no customers are
willing to buy may require a monetary outlay, and so the total
cost curve may intersect the ruble axis at a positive amount.
As quality is improved, both total revenue and total costs increase, but the slope of each may change repeatedly. As a
result, the monopolist's total profit may reach a number of
local maxima such that a movement from any one of them
would reduce total profit. It is not clear, therefore, that a
monopolist would arrive at his maximum maximorum profit
level, or greatest possible profit.

We should note that if a monopolist sells his commodity
in more than one market or if he can differentiate his customers
into a number of separate groups, then the quality of product
that maximizes his profit in one market may not be the quality
that maximizes his profit in the other markets. Hence the
monopolist may produce different qualities of the same commodity, and he may engage in quality discrimination similar
to the price discrimination of Western markets.

DUOPOLY

Suppose that only two firms produce a certain commodity.
If either firm alters the quality of its product, then the customer

demand for each firm's product will shift. Let us refer to the
two firms as Firm A and Firm B, and let us suppose that Firm
A changes the quality of its product while Firm B keeps its
quality constant. If Firm A raises the quality of its product,
it will be able to sell more than it could previously, Firm B
will not be able to sell as much as it would previously, and
the total amount sold will increase. If Firm A reduces the
quality of its product, it will not be able to sell as much as
it could previously, Firm B will be able to sell more than it
could previously, and the total amount sold will decrease.

In this situation, a type of warfare could develop in which
each firm would seek to produce a better quality product than
its competitor. With the price having been set by the central
planners, however, such warfare would result in a decrease
in the total profit of each duopolist. In view of this, the duopolists might decide to collude concerning the quality of their
products. Such collusion could occur as the result of face-to-
face negotiations or it could develop tacitly as each observed
the other's behavior. In either case, the collusion could result in the same type of behavior as that of the monopolist already described, or it could be interrupted by periods of warfare as each decided to fight for a larger share of the market.
In the process of determining market shares, one firm could
become dominant and acquire a greater total profit solely because of its negotiating ability or willingness to fight vis-à-vis
the other firm.

OLIGOPOLY

If several firms compete in a certain product market, then
the quality decisions of any one firm affect the sales volume
of each of the others. Because of this sales interdependence,
each firm may face a kinked demand curve for its product. If
one oligopolist raises the quality of his product all the other
firms may be forced to copy his example or lose the bulk of
their customers. Hence if an oligopolist raises the quality
of his product, the amount he can sell may not change much.
If he lowers the quality of his product, on the other hand, most
of his customers may desert to his competitors. Therefore,
the situation depicted in Figure 6 may be relevant for the
oligopolist, where the quantity the oligopolist can sell is a
function of the quality of his product, and where the oligopolist
will tend to produce a commodity of the quality QL_1.

A quality leader may emerge in such a situation. The leader may set quality standards that the other firms tend to follow. If another firm should raise the quality of its product above these standards--thereby violating the tacit collusion under which they all operate--the leader could respond by raising the quality of its product. As a result, the profit of each firm would be below its original level. Each of the non-leaders would realize, due to this punishment, that it could maximize its profit only by producing a commodity of the same quality as the leader's commodity.

MONOPOLISTIC COMPETITION

Suppose that a firm must obtain permission from the central planners in order to shift into the production of new commodities. Suppose that the central planners are reluctant to permit such dissatisfaction, preferring instead to restrict each market to a given number of suppliers. Let us consider such a market where the number of suppliers is large but fixed. In this case, if the central planners set a certain price, P_1 so as to clear the market for the commodity, any one of the producers, Firm A, can act as if it controls a segment of the market. If the greatest amount that all producers, behaving as perfect competitors, are willing to supply is Q_1, and if the greatest amount that all firms other than A are willing to supply is Q_X, then Firm A controls the market for $Q_1 - Q_X$.

Firm A can now reduce the quality of its commodity in the knowledge that a demand will exist for its debased product. True, customers will first seek to obtain the commodity from Firm A's competitors. If the latter keep to the government price, however, the competitors will have to turn away some of the customers. The shape of the demand curve for the debased product will depend upon the intensity of demand of those particular customers who have been rejected. Hence it may vary from one time period to another. Any one of the producers, such as Firm A, may act as a monopolist toward these rejected customers in deciding upon the degree of quality debasement that will maximize its profit. In this decision process, the monopolistic competitor, like the monopolist discussed above, may experience the difficulty that a number of local profit maxima exist and the movement towards the maximum maximorum profit may not constantly increase its total profit.

FIGURE 6

The Oligopolist's Demand Curve
with Centrally Set Prices

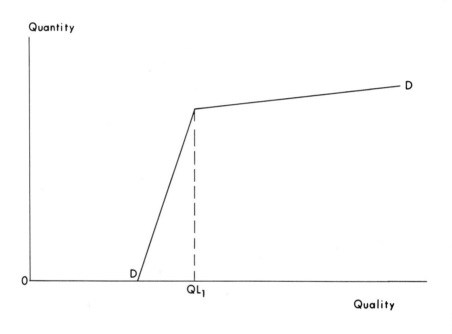

Each of the monopolistic competitors may find it in its interest to reduce product quality. The result may be that customers receive commodities significantly inferior to the commodity whose price central planners originally fixed, while each supplier may receive a total profit in excess of the amount it would have received initially.

QUALITY STANDARDS

If a nation contains monopoly, duopoly, oligopoly, or monopolistic competition, it is not enough for central planners to set prices. As the above analyses indicate, they may also have to set specific and detailed quality standards. Only in the case of monopolistic competition did an excess demand exist for a commodity, and in no case did any of the firms produce an excess supply. Hence central planners could not use the existence of excess demand or excess supply as an indication that quality had been debased. For central planners to respond to quality debasement by lowering the market price is not a reasonable solution if central planners desire production of a better quality product.

Implementation of quality standards may be a difficult task. Enterprise personnel may be involved in discussions concerning quality standards and, if so, they may advocate those types of standards that they believe can be violated without such violations being detected readily. Faced with such conduct, central planners might not be able to obtain adequate information on which to base their standards. To be completely effective, standards would have to deal with every aspect of each commodity that could be debased. A comprehensive inspection system would have to be capable of detecting any infractions of the established standards.

An alternative solution might be for central planners to permit free entry into any industry. If any enterprise could produce any commodity it wished or if any group of individuals could create a new firm whenever it wished, then a monopolist, duopolist, oligopolist, or monopolistic competitor might not behave in the manner described above for fear that a higher-than-normal profit would attract new competitors. It is not clear what specific institutional regulations could best provide for such free entry. Necessary modifications in the nation's legal, financial, and planning structure might be opposed because of their effect on other aspects of the economy. The

optimal criterion for entry is also not clear. A higher-than-
normal profit would not necessarily indicate the existence of
a market imperfection. Such profit might be the result of
exceptional initiative, exertion, skill or care; and this possibility further complicates the solution of additional suppliers.
Potential competitors might be barred by cost considerations
alone. Economies of large-scale production, for example,
might effectively limit the market to one firm.

The comments in this chapter concerning the possible behavior of monopolists, duopolists, oligopolists, and monopolistic competitors resemble analyses of these kinds of market
imperfections in Western economies. A fundamental difference,
of course, is that within the framework of central price setting
each enterprise may increase its profit by debasing quality
rather than by increasing its prices. With this difference in
mind, insights meaningful in this second planning framework
can be found in works such as those by R. L. Bishop, [1] E. H.
Chamberlin, [2] W. Fellner, [3] K. W. Rothschild, [4] G. J. Stigler, [5]
P. M. Sweezy, [6] and R. Triffin. [7] The possibility of such market imperfections complicates the task of setting prices centrally and so may detract significantly from the desirability
of this second planning framework.

DIFFERENTIAL PRICING

The Russian leadership has decided that differential pricing should be followed in the U.S.S.R. Low-cost producers,
such as Firm A in Figure 7, will be paid a lower-than-normal
price for their output while high-cost producers, such as
Firm C, will receive a price that is higher than normal.

From a short-run point of view, it seems that differential
pricing will result in inefficient production. If each firm seeks
to maximize its profit, it will expand production to the point
where the price it receives equals its marginal cost. Hence
Firms A, B, and C, being paid P_A, P_B, and P_C respectively,
will produce Q_A, Q_B, and Q_C respectively. If Firm A's output were increased by one unit while Firm C's output were
decreased by one unit, total output would remain unchanged
while total costs would fall, since A's marginal cost at Q_A is
below C's marginal cost at Q_C. Hence differential pricing
seems to lead to inefficient production.

From a long-run point of view, however, differential
pricing may be a reasonable means of encouraging the economic

FIGURE 7

Determination of Output with Differential Pricing

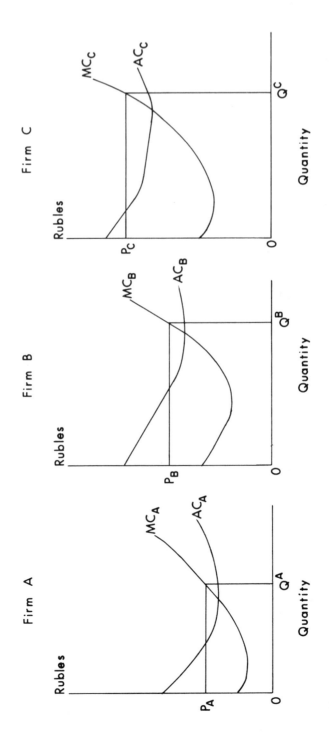

development of a nation's low-income regions. Production costs may be affected over time by the level of economic activity in the individual firms or in the region as a whole. The individual firms may benefit through the production of larger volumes. This may occur, for example, if some learning by doing is involved in the production process. As high-cost producers increase the volume of their output, they may experience a decrease in their average and marginal expenses over time. Both the average-cost curve and the marginal-cost curve of Firm C may fall as time passes. Economic development may be viewed as a cumulative advance in which the initial steps are the most difficult and least profitable. Hence the initial steps should be subsidized. Existence of external economies may mean that an expansion of one firm, say Firm C, may have a stimulating impact on other economic activities of the depressed region. From this point of view, differential to pursue. It may be applied to the purchase prices firms pay for their inputs as well as to the prices they receive for their output. Central planners may charge firms in a depressed region a lower-than-normal interest rate for the capital they use. Firms in advanced regions may be charged a higher interest rate.

Differential pricing may be considered a necessary and powerful weapon in the nation's struggle to stimulate its economically depressed regions. It may also be used as a means of achieving a greater equality of incomes among regions. In fact, it is this pursuit of greater income equality that is usually mentioned in the Soviet press in support of differential pricing. What is clear in either case is that, in using differential pricing, central planners must forecast the impact of alternative sets of prices on current production volumes and on future production costs. Such forecasting of the effects of differential pricing must add to the difficulty and complexity of the tasks facing central planners.

NOTES

1. R. L. Bishop, "Duopoly: Collusion or Warfare?" American Economic Review, (1960).

2. E. H. Chamberlin, Theory of Monopolistic Competition (Cambridge: Harvard University Press, 1933).

3.   W. Fellner, Competition among the Few (New York: Alfred A. Knopf, Inc. , 1949).

4.   K. W. Rothschild, "Price Theory and Oligopoly," Economic Journal, LVII (1947).

5.   G. J. Stigler, "The Kinky Oligopoly Demand Curve and Rigid Prices," Journal of Political Economy, LV (1947).

6.   P. M. Sweezy, "Demand under Condition of Oligopoly," Journal of Political Economy, XLVII (1939).

7.   R. Triffin, Monopolistic Competition and General Equilibrium Theory, (Cambridge: Harvard University Press, 1940).

9

RUSSIAN REFORMS PRIOR TO 1965

Let us first consider decision making within the Soviet political leadership. Here it is important to note that the pattern of investment among different types of industry as well as between agriculture and industry has been determined by a few politicians at the summit of the governmental pyramid. At this level, we can see a distinct shift at the death of Stalin from supreme decision making by one man to a situation where open conflict has taken place over such investment decisions. Malenkov's new emphasis in 1953 on more investment in consumer durables was opposed by heavy industry supporters like Bulganin and Kozlov, by defense-minded politicians, and also by Khrushchev, who advocated a major shift toward investment in agriculture. Sidney Ploss[1] has emphasized that throughout the 1950's and 1960's such controversies have been carried from the Presidium and Council of Ministers to the Central Committee of the Communist Party where in vigorous debate and actual balloting the investment policies of the U.S.S.R. have been determined. It is here that the decisions were made to undertake an intensive development of the chemical industry, to shift from steel to aluminum in the construction of many products, and, more recently, to adopt the Brezhnev program of an expanded investment in land reclamation and the mechanization of agriculture.

In the city of Moscow there are bureaucrats whose job has been to construct itemized plans and issue the detailed instructions which bring the desires of the politicians into actuality. The work of these bureaucrats must be coordinated if the activities of each firm are to fit in smoothly with those of every other firm. Have the politicians been satisfied with such coordination among the central planners? In 1947, the responsibility for the formulation of plans for the allocation of products

among firms and consumers was divided between a newly
created State Committee for Materials Supply known as Gossnab
and the older agency known as Gosplan. Responsibilities of
Gossnab for consumers' goods were transferred to still another
agency in 1951. In 1953, both of these agencies for material
supply were merged with Gosplan. This situation lasted only
for two years. In 1955, Gosplan was confined to the construction of long-term plans. Responsibility for annual plans was
placed in the hands of a new body, the State Economic Commission or Gosek. In 1960, responsibilities for construction of
long-term plans were this time removed from Gosplan and
given to the State Scientific-Economic Council (Gosekonomsovet),
while for the first time Gosplan was to be responsible solely
for annual plans. In 1962, Gosekonomsovet was abolished and
once more Gosplan was responsible for integrating all national
plans. These drastic structural changes illustrate the difficulty the Soviet political leadership has experienced merely
in coordinating its central planners.

When we examine another group of planners, we encounter
bureaucrats whose duties are more those of technicians. Until
1957, these administrators occupied offices in Moscow as well,
where they were divided into separate ministries numbering
from twenty to thirty. A sweeping reform in 1957 shifted the
responsibilities of these men from Moscow to regional sovnarkhozy. The reason for the shift was proclaimed to be
acute dissatisfaction with the previous structure of interindus-
trial coordination. A gap existed between the central planners
first described and these technician-bureaucrats. Each ministry feared that it would not be given adequate consideration by
the central planners in the question of how much material
supplies it should receive from other ministries. If it was to
perform satisfactorily, each ministry had to be confident that
its inputs would arrive, that they would arrive on time, and
that they would be of the necessary quality.

Hence, a tendency rapidly developed for each ministry
to construct informal material balances of its own for the
activities for which it was responsible. A principal goal of
each ministry was to minimize the inputs which it would need
from other ministries. Each ministry provided the central
planners with a consolidated estimate of the total output of
each commodity which that ministry could produce and of the
inputs it would need from other ministries. The planners,
however, could not determine the extent to which the ministry
was intending to produce for its own use those inputs which
other ministries could provide more cheaply--either because

some other ministry specialized in certain inputs or because
it had a firm nearer to the user than the first ministry did.
Examples of ridiculously long transportation hauls which more
interministry coordination could have avoided have been cited
by many Soviet economists. Inefficiency occurred not only because of this type of ministerial independence, but also because
by-products useful in other ministries were often discarded.
Aside from the personal interest of ministerial officials, we
see the major problem that one ministry really could not estimate the cost of its autarchy to the economy as a whole. It
had no way of knowing how cheaply another ministry could produce or deliver its inputs. Unaware of such costs, each ministry could truly believe that its policy of self-reliance was
serving the national interest since this policy was preventing
major disruptions due to insufficient or inappropriate inputs;
and in some cases this policy probably was serving the national
interest. In 1964, V.S. Nemchinov, a Russian economist expressed the following view:

> The situation here is analogous to the one that exist-
> ed with respect to steam engines at the dawn of the
> Industrial Revolution. In Newcomen's time, before
> Watt's governor was invented, the movement of
> steam in a steam engine was controlled by having a
> person pull the valve by hand at the right moment.
> Such a situation can no more be tolerated in run-
> ning an economy than in running a machine. [2]

The 1957 reform abolished the government ministries and
replaced them with over 100 regional planning groups or sovnarkhozy. For the economic steam engine, constant manual
control was still to be necessary--it was simply to be a different type of manual control. But the economy still did not
run smoothly. In September, 1965, in a speech before the
Plenary Session of the CPSU Central Committee, Kosygin
discussed this sovnarkhoz reform.

> In the course of time major shortcomings began
> to appear in the management of industry. Guid-
> ance of a branch of industry that was a unified
> whole in respect to its production technology
> was scattered among numerous economic re-
> gions and ended up totally disrupted . . . The
> sovnarkhozy do not have the necessary skilled
> cadres to supervise their many branches of in-
> dustry. [3]

Economic coordination along regional lines seemed to be
even more inefficient than coordination along branch or type of

industry lines. Now each region tended to become an independent, self-sufficient unit--in order to avoid reliance upon other regional authorities who would place the interests of their own enterprises first. Regional autarchy developed in the place of ministerial autarchy. To coordinate the economic activities of the regional units, the central planners needed the same type of detailed information they had needed previously, and they experienced the same difficulty in analyzing such information and formulating decisions based on it. In addition, there was now no single group thoroughly familiar with one particular industry and capable of coordinating the affairs such as scientific research and technological innovation peculiar to that industry. The number of sovnarkhozy was cut to forty-seven in an effort to overcome the most obvious inefficiencies caused by a small area trying to fill all its own needs. In 1963, eighteen new councils and planning commissions were created, each responsible for several of the existing sovnarkhozy in a further attempt to improve coordination. In 1965, the entire sovnarkhoz system was abolished.

THE PROFIT REFORM MOVEMENT

At the Twenty-second Congress of the Communist Party in October, 1961, Khrushchev indicated that a completely different type of reform might be pursued in an effort to overcome the coordination problems experienced by his nation in its central planning. "We must elevate the importance of profit and profitability. In order to have enterprises fulfill their plans better, they should be given more opportunity to dispose of their profits, to use them more extensively to encourage good work of their personnel, and to extend production."[4] In the following year, discussion of this subject increased in the Soviet press. In his report to the November, 1962, Plenary Session of the CPSU Central Committee, Khrushchev commented on the discussion of a wide range of economic questions that had developed recently in Pravda, Izvestiya, and Ekonomicheskaya gazeta. "Many valuable proposals," he said, "have been made in the course of the discussion . . . The planning agencies and the Economics Institute of the U.S.S.R. Academy of Sciences should be assigned to study these proposals carefully."[5]

In conformity with this attitude, an extremely important commission was organized. It was composed of members of

the following: the U.S.S.R. Academy of Sciences' Economics
Division, governmental planning and economic agencies, particular enterprises, the editorial boards of certain newspapers
and journals, and educational institutions. Discussions within
the commission and recommendations by the commission cov-
ered the whole field of central planning, including such topics
as improvement in the indices used in planning and evaluating
the work of each enterprise, methods for encouraging more
effective utilization of capital, means of stimulating technological progress, and the expansion of the role of profits.

Early in the national discussion of profit reforms it was
generally recognized that the relative prices for different goods
and services would become much more important than they had
been previously. If each individual enterprise was to be granted
freedom to alter its inputs, outputs, or production technology
solely on its own initiative, and if in such alteration it was
being urged by national leaders and its own self-interest to
maximize profits, then the pattern of prices that it faced at
present and the pattern it estimated for the future would affect
its decisions. Hence a series of questions concerning prices
attained new significance. Could prices and profit maximization by themselves result in optimal resource allocation, or
did successful operation of the economy require other indices
for planning and evaluation as well? Should the individual enterprise be restricted in the scope of its decisions, and should
certain areas such as investment decisions be reserved for
determination by central authorities? What should a price represent? What factors should enter its determination? In particular, should land rent and interest on capital be included in
price; or should prices, for example, be differentiated so that
in any industry those enterprises having poorer management,
land, or capital would receive higher prices to compensate
them for their higher costs? Should prices be changed frequently to reflect changes in production conditions such as
cost reduction innovations or quality improvements? Most
important, could any organization, in practice, formulate and
revise prices rapidly enough to prevent incorrect prices from
causing incorrect decisions at the enterprise level?

In Chapter 7, I have already discussed Soviet views concerning the various possible profit maximization criteria.
Soviet economic thought on this issue has been confused, and
inappropriate criteria could deprive profit maximization of
much of its potential impact. Soviet criticism of the profit
criterion has focused on points other than this, however. In a
1962 article, Gatovsky stressed the division between the current

operation of an enterprise on the one hand and investment decisions on the other. Although appropriate for the former,
profit maximization was inappropriate, he believed, for the
latter. Under capitalism, investment funds move towards
those sectors of the economy enjoying higher than average profits. In the U.S.S.R., however, investment funds, for reasons
not specified by Gatovsky, can be better allocated through direct intervention by central planners. In addition to this restriction on the role of profit, Gatovsky also felt that restrictions should be placed on the importance of profit maximization
in a firm's decisions concerning current operations. "Life
confirms at every turn that for us the level of profitability can
by no means serve as a single absolute criterion of an enterprise's success and replace the other value indicators of production, not to mention the physical ones."[6] He referred to
the volume of output, the mix of products, and the quality of
the product as indicators still useful in planning and evaluation. Why should the role of profit be restricted even at the
enterprise level? Gatovsky, although not answering this question directly, implied that price formation was a considerable
part of the answer.

> One of the prerequisites for heightening the role
> and significance of profits is further price adjust-
> ment. . . . Evidence indicates that it is not only
> periodic general revisions of prices that are needed
> but also systematic current measures to adjust
> prices . . . If prices are not revised for a long time,
> then great lack of coordination inevitably arises in
> profits . . . The existing price-setting methods
> often do not create an incentive for an enterprise to
> produce new machines or machines with improved
> qualities. . . . An incorrect price structure not
> only neutralizes the stimulating role of profits but
> even creates a situation in which profits have a
> negative influence on production.[7]

Thus as early as 1962 doubts were voiced as to the ability
of governmental agencies to formulate and revise prices accurately enough to justify reliance on profit maximization.

On December 13, 1963, at the Plenary Session of the
CPSU Central Committee, Khrushchev again stressed "We
must display the highest exactitude towards the quality of manufactured goods in general. Evidently we should introduce a
system whereby factories and firms are directly responsible
to the consumer for the quality of their output."[8] On July 1,
1964, a new system was introduced on an experimental basis

at the Bolshevichka and Mayak garment firms located respectively in the cities of Moscow and Gorky. M. Kuznetsova, the
chief economist and assistant general director of the Bolshevichka enterprise, has described this system.

> The right has been granted to us to compose plans
> on the basis of orders from the trade organizations
> and to determine for ourselves the volume of pro-
> duction, the volume of output sales, the necessary
> materials, and the wage fund. The only report
> indices are now the volume of output sold on orders
> and the percentage of profit. Now it is not the eco-
> nomic council that imposes the assortment on us,
> but we who inform the economic council of what we
> are going to be making in our shops. [9]

In October, 1964, G. Fokin, director of the Central Department Store, and L. Geller, senior consultant for quality of
goods at that store, voiced their approval of the new system.
"In our opinion the large department stores must be freed from
the tutelage of the wholesale depots and given an opportunity
to order goods, within the limits of their funds, directly from
the textile, footwear, garment, and knitwear enterprises. Our
department store now has direct communications with the Bolshevichka Garment Production Association, and this experience
has justified itself completely."[10]

It should be mentioned that not all indicators appeared favorable, and not all observers considered the new system to be
flawless or perhaps even superior to the traditional methods.
"All the basic indices of the [Bolshevichka] firm's work were
worse [initially] than in 1963--profits were lower, as were
production volume and labor productivity, and production costs
were higher. It took some time to prove that the direct ties
were not to blame in this case."[11] In an article quoted above,
M. Kuznetsova remarked that representatives of the U.S.S.R.
Ministry of Finance visited the Bolshevichka firm and consequently sent a letter denouncing the transition to the new system
to the Chairman of the U.S.S.R. Council of the National Economy. In spite of such doubts, in October, 1964, the Presidium
of the U.S.S.R. Council of Ministers charged the U.S.S.R.
Council of the National Economy with preparing a draft resolution on spreading the experiences of Bolshevichka and Mayak
to other light-industry enterprises. On October 19 and 20,
a special session of the Council of the National Economy was
convened to discuss the four-month-old experiment. "Those
who spoke in the subsequent discussion stressed the need for
increasing the number of enterprises in light industry that

work according to direct contracts with trade organizations and stores." [12] The experiment was judged, by this Council, to have been a success.

This initial experiment was truly a most radical shift in that not only was decision making decentralized on the basis of profit maximization, but also the framework for price formation was completely changed. The two large firms involved in the experiment were to set their own retail prices on the basis of their own individual and independent evaluation of the market. V. Veselovsky has emphasized this aspect of the experiment. He has cited, as an example, a case where the two firms decided to improve the quality of one line of inexpensive suits. With the accompanying rise in production cost, "inexpensive, popular suits have proved unprofitable. What is the answer? In the opinion of the firms' officials, the prices of the expensive suits (few of which are bought) must be reduced, and the prices of the cheaper suits should be raised 3 to 5 rubles. . . . No sooner said than done, considering that the directors of these firms have been granted the right to establish retail prices." [13]

On July 1, 1965, exactly one year after the initial experiment was begun, all the garment and footwear factories of Moscow and several other cities started to operate according to direct contracts with their purchasers and also with their suppliers. This new experiment embraced some 400 enterprises. In several respects the new experiment seemed to offer considerable improvement over traditional methods. According to an article by O. Lacis each firm now planned its assortment of goods in such a way as to correspond more fully to the desires of those who would receive them. The firm accepted orders for goods on a contract basis and the direct contacts between supplier and purchaser enabled information concerning the capabilities of suppliers and the wishes of purchasers to flow in more accurate detail than when communication channels ran through the central planning bureaucracy. Fines for failure to meet delivery dates were considerable and reduced profits, which now meant a reduction in the enterprise fund and bonuses.

However, several major shortcomings existed in the July 1, 1965, experiment. Lacis noted that while garment factories could make the same demands for appropriate goods from textile factories, the latter could not carry on the chain of direct contacts and responsibilities. Those who supplied spun fiber, cotton, wool, artificial fiber, dyes, and equipment--all these were free from the local responsibility of the new system.

Hence textile suppliers were limited in their responses to garment firms and the whole system could not achieve its maximum impact.

Of more importance, Lacis criticized the retreat to the formation of prices by governmental agencies rather than by individual firms.

The experiment disclosed more clearly than ever before the imperfect condition of prices. In particular, scarce output exists not per se, but only at the given price . . . It is no accident that the management of Bolshevichka, which has the most experience in operating in the new way, is demanding that the enterprises' participation in the establishment of prices be expanded. . . . In the second resolution of the U.S.S.R. Council of the National Economy--the one that expanded the experiment-- this right was no longer provided for. Bolshevichka was deprived of it, along with the newcomers. After that what was the point of the experiment? After all, there had been no instances to cast doubt on the usefulness of this step. On the other hand, there are countless examples to confirm the imperfectness of the present system of price formation.[14]

During this initial experimental period, a great deal of debate arose in the Soviet press concerning the experiments and the proper framework for central planning. A variety of possible improvements in this framework were suggested. Professor Liberman, for example, stressed the need for greater flexibility in the economy and suggested in one article that inventories or reserves should be increased to assist in achieving this flexibility.

Wholesale trade is impossible without reserves. The creation of such reserves is a matter of enormous importance, for they could allow us at last to solve the problem of reliability and of greater maneuverability of the supply system, something we have been thinking about and struggling for so hard. A changed approach is essential. I shall explain by a simple example. We are accustomed to thinking that a cinema must be crowded to capacity, a train must not have a single empty compartment, all rooms in a hotel must be occupied. The work of the public-catering and service establishments is unthinkable

to us any other way at present. But is this really
economical and sensible? We forget that such work
"without waste" in the long run involves enormous
waste to society, to you and me. Much of your
time and ours, time that could be productive and
socially useful, is wasted in red tape, waiting,
and queuing up. And how can we calculate the
senseless waste of nerves, of simple health?
I repeat that there is no need to be afraid of reserves, for these will pay off a hundred times
over![15]

For many advocates of a new system, profit maximization
was not the obvious alternative to maximization of the traditional index of gross output. Instead, some advocated the
"normative value of processing" or "N.V.P." These writers
criticized the gross-output criterion most severely. "Above
all, with identical labor outlays at enterprises, the volume of
their gross output may increase or decrease depending on the
cost of the initial materials they are using and the planned rate
of profit . . . Calculating the enterprise's output by using the
gross output indicator does not stimulate fulfillment of the plan
for product assortment because the enterprise has an interest
in producing the items with the largest material inputs."[16]
They felt that an index of value added could solve the basic
shortcomings of the traditional system. The N.V.P. would be
equal to gross output minus profit and minus those basic materials and purchased semimanufactures that do not lose their
consumable properties yet are included with little alteration in
the finished product. Those inputs that do lose their consumable properties, such as fuel and power, would be included in
N.V.P. "The distorted incentive for enterprises to produce
items that consume much material and are highly profitable
is thereby removed."[17] At least implicit in this argument is
the belief that the size of an enterprise's profits is without
economic meaning--because profit depends upon wholesale
prices and these prices are determined arbitrarily by central
planners. Wholesale prices, and therefore profits, do not
systematically reflect usefulness, production costs, or scar-
city.

Beginning in 1961 certain enterprises were shifted to a
maximization of N.V.P. and N.V.P. per laborer, particularly
in the former Tatar Economic Council. In a 1964 article, the
First Secretary of the Tatar Province Party Committee expressed praise for this system of planning and evaluation and
urged its widespread consideration.[18] Important voices spoke

against this index, however. The Deputy Director of the U.S.S.R.
Central Statistical Administration, for example, stated
"It is impossible to agree with the new index, the so-called
normative value of processing (N.V.P.) defended by Comrade
Tabeyev. . . . Each of these elements of expenditures has an
individual economic meaning. But the sum of them, by virtue
of the arbitrary selection of items, becomes meaningless."[19]
The division of purchased inputs between those to be included
and those to be excluded would in practice deprive the N.V.P.
criterion of the precision and clarity that such an index must
possess. Nemchinov also criticized the N.V.P. and, in the
same article, discussed in detail the questions of price formation and the need for decentralized decision making. He
emphasized that

> No superior agency can know the internal produc-
> tion resources and conditions as well as the enter-
> prise itself does . . . Each enterprise should
> present to the planning agencies its preliminary
> proposals as to the conditions on which it is pre-
> pared to fill a given plan assignment for delivery
> of a product (with assortment, quality, delivery
> date, and price indicated). The economic and
> planning agencies should distribute their contracts
> only among the enterprises that propose condi-
> tions that are most advantageous to the national
> economy as a whole. . . . Everything that is
> advantageous and beneficial to the national eco-
> nomy as a whole ought to be beneficial also to
> the enterprise--the operational unit--that is
> carrying out the particular part of the plan. This
> principle can be ensured if the plan assignment
> becomes a plan contract and if the basic condi-
> tions for filling the contract are established, par-
> ticularly if the price is acceptable to both the
> planning agency and the enterprise.[20]

The planning framework within which Nemchinov saw profit maximization as the optimal goal is quite different from the
planning framework envisaged by the advocates of N.V.P. For
Nemchinov, prices should have definite meaning; the profit
margins that prices affect should have definite meaning. Individual enterprises should have a role in price formation. "A
more flexible and improved procedure for planning prices would
make it possible to eliminate completely any contradictions
between price and plan. Only in this event will prices be able
to perform their basic role as an economic regulator . . ."[21]

Advocates of N. V. P. did perceive the extremely important fact that if the correctness of prices and their flexibility to meet changing circumstances were not present in the economy, then profits and profit maximization would become meaningless. Nemchinov also saw this. The real issue at dispute was the possibility of developing a successful method for price formation in the U.S.S.R. today.

A number of Soviet economists have expressed confidence in the ability of flexible prices to call forth quality improvements in goods previously produced and to encourage the development of new products--as well as to lead to cost reductions and the production of the proper amounts of each good. [22] As discussed earlier, the problem of quality and new products--if central planners are setting prices--requires even more technical knowledge than does the problem of coordinating production plans when quality and types of products are constant. It is not surprising, therefore, to see comments about increasing the role of the individual enterprise in this aspect of price formation. An engineer in an automobile plant wrote a letter to Pravda in which he stated, "The consumer must have the first word in deciding the question of whether a higher price should or should not be paid for quality. For it is precisely he who derives a saving from new machinery." [23] An economist in another plant wrote, "In order for the market to assist in controlling the assortment and quality of products, it is necessary for enterprises and marketing and trade organizations to have maximum autonomy on questions of concluding contracts to supply and sell their items, and also to a certain degree on setting the price of the products being sold and bought." [24] In an article on "The Independence of the Enterprise and Economic Stimuli," two prominent economists have written,

> In our opinion it is advisable gradually to abolish centralized control over the numbers of personnel and the wage fund. . . . Enterprises themselves should be granted the right to correct the plan for output of goods by agreement with the consumers (those who place the orders). The plan should be based on the customers' orders. Perhaps in establishing prices in planned fashion they should be considered only an obligatory upper limit, and the sale of goods below the fixed prices should be permitted. On the other hand, when goods of the best quality, or goods that have better consumer qualities than provided for by the standards, are produced, enterprises should be allowed to set prices in agreement with the customer. [25]

It is interesting to note the existence of such views even in
1964 when the profit experiment was limited to the Bolshevichka
and Mayak firms. Among the highest authorities, these views
were apparently not powerful enough to overcome confidence in
the cental planners and, as mentioned above, the July 1, 1965,
revision rescinded the freedom of individual enterprises to
alter their prices. Since 1965, debate has continued concerning the proper role of local firms in price determination. Various suggestions have been presented, such as the creation of
a two-tier price system where customers may pay the lower
price for inferior products. Financial penalties for inappropriate commodities or late deliveries have been discussed
earlier in this book. Clearly the development of price-setting
techniques has presented a problem of great concern to the
Soviet leadership.

     Another interesting aspect of the reform program was the
incentive system for encouraging the management and workers
within each firm to adhere to the rules. It was generally considered that to urge or require everyone to maximize profit
(or some profit ratio) by reducing costs and increasing output
was not enough by itself: such appeals had to be supported by
a system of bonuses for successful performance. Over the
years a system of bonus payments had developed based on the
fulfillment of many indicators, a main one being fulfillment of
the gross-output plan. In addition, the enterprise fund was
formed out of profits (or out of savings from reducing unit costs
in the case of planned-loss enterprises); and this fund was used
to improve cultural and living conditions of the firm's workers.
Now the question was raised of replacing the large number of
bonus norms by the one index, profit.[26] At one point, Liberman
suggested that the incentive norm be based on the level of profitability, but that the bonus could be expressed as a share of
the wage fund. For instance, at a profitability rate of 10 per
cent, an amount equalling 7 per cent of the wage fund might be
deducted from profits into the incentive fund, and at a profitability rate of 20 per cent, say 12 per cent of the amount of
the wage fund might be deducted into this fund. In any case,
"enterprises should have a long-term normative for incentive,
which will not be revised every time the enterprise surpasses
it. The enterprise should always be sure that a share of its
success will be retained by the collective that earned the success."[27]

     As the reforms have spread across Soviet industries, a
variety of success criteria have been implemented. Liberman's
advocacy of profitability has been followed, in that for each

percentage point in the firm's rate of profitability, the firm will receive a specified percentage increase in its total wage and salary fund. The rate of profitability is defined here as total profits as a percentage of the value of fixed and circulating capital. Some groups of firms have received a bonus based on increases in total profits as well as the bonus based on profitability. In this case, a 1 per cent increase in a firm's total profits will result in a specified increase in the firm's total wage and salary fund. Other groups of firms have received bonuses based on increases in their sales volumes, calculated in the same manner. Various combinations of these success criteria have been applied. Two other funds, in addition to the wage and salary fund, have received supplements based on one or more of profitability, increases in total profits, and increases in total sales: the social-cultural fund, which is used for such purposes as housing and clubs for the firm's personnel, and the production-development fund, which is used to finance investment in machinery and equipment.

In October, 1965, the Council of Ministers and the Central Committee of the Communist Party expressed their view that the reforms should be extended throughout Soviet industry. In the first quarter of 1966, 43 industrial enterprises were shifted to the new system; in the third quarter, another 430 firms were transferred. By January of 1969 nearly all Soviet industry was supposed to be operating within the new planning framework.

Most of what has been said in this chapter up to this point has referred to the Soviet economy in general. Looking at agriculture, we see that economic reforms could affect the agricultural production process in two ways. First, they could result in more and better industrial inputs for agriculture. In the first part of this book, we noted some of the shortcomings in the Stalin-Khrushchev system of supplying agriculture with industrial products. It is possible that an alternative planning and administrative framework might be able to conquer these shortcomings and supply chemical fertilizers, drainage and irrigation equipment, and farm machinery that would be better able to assist farm workers in their daily operations. A second way that economic reforms could affect the agricultural production process would be through changing the planning and administrative framework for each individual farm. Decentralization of decision making in agriculture has been as much a part of the economic reform discussions as industrial decentralization has been; many of the writers quoted above were thinking as much about agriculture as they were about industry when they emphasized profit maximization and local initiative and responsibility. In a resolution in March, 1964, the CPSU Central Committee and the U.S.S.R. Council of Ministers declared that the composition of plans for the development of agricultural production must begin directly on the collective and state farms and must be carried out with an eye to the actual production conditions and possibilities of each farm. They stated that "Serious shortcomings have been permitted in the planning of state purchases of farm products. The production orientation of the farm, its specialization, is not always taken into account in fixing the plans for the sale of products to the state by collective and state farms."[28] Purchases by the state of agricultural produce were still to be based on annual plans, but the requests and advice of each farm were now to exert a decisive influence on the formation of these plans. One concrete revision was "To consider as no longer in force Point 5 of the March 9, 1955, resolution of the CPSU Central Committee and the U.S.S.R. Council of Ministers On Revising the Practice of Planning Agriculture, which grants the district executive committees the right to review the sowing and animal husbandry plans of the collective farms and to return these plans for revision if there are disagreements with the collective farms."[29]

Official encouragement increased for decision making and initiative on the part of each farm, rather than for passive acceptance of stereotyped decrees and specific plans decided upon by the central planners. In March, 1965, Brezhnev presented an important revision of agricultural administration. The plan for state grain purchases was reduced (from 4 to 3.4 billion poods); this plan for 3.4 billion poods was declared to be fixed and unalterable for each year of the 1965-1970 period. Any state purchases above this minimum level were to be the result not of central decrees but rather of local responses to a set of prices. In 1965, for example, the prices for sales of wheat and rye above the basic plan were set 50 per cent higher than the basic purchase prices. "Our experience in increasing the production of cotton and sugar beets convincingly shows how important it is to observe a correct price policy for agricultural products."[30] Under Stalin a two-level system of prices also existed; but the present practice appears to be geared to a much greater degree to the active response of individual farms and the price structure appears to be a flexible structure which will be altered to shape these responses indirectly rather than through overt intervention. In regard to increasing the output of livestock products and expansion of the fodder

crops necessary for this, Brezhnev declared, "Let the collective farmers, state farm workers, and agricultural specialists
decide how to do this themselves. They know local conditions
best, and it is more apparent to them what to plant on their
lands and what to feed their livestock."[31] Brezhnev also presented a new approach to agricultural investment which was
similar in its decentralization emphasis to the crop and livestock planning described above. "We must abandon excessive
regimentation in the distribution of capital investments and subsidies to the state farms and shift the state farms to full economic independence (khozraschet) as soon as possible. The
state farms will retain for their own uses the profits they receive . . ."[32]

Does such a planning and administrative framework permit enough local flexibility? Several prominent writers feel
that it does not. They have urged that even the basic or minimum plan for state purchases be abolished, so that farms
would be completely free to determine all of their crop and
livestock sales. They fear that central planners, in their collaboration concerning the state plan, will in practice ignore
the advice of individual farms. To prevent this, all such
decision-making power must be given to the farms. Nearly
all Soviet observers reject price determination in the market
as the best formula for state purchases. Since much agricultural produce is already sold at prices determined in the market, the government operations here are seen as a balancing
factor to prevent sudden shortages of certain goods and to provide a guaranteed market for agricultural produce as well as
a guaranteed supply for city inhabitants. The writers urging
an abolition of state purchase plans see prices and careful
changes in prices as a lever which the government can use to
achieve these goals; and they consider prices to be the best
lever because in such a framework it will be the individual
farms who will make the decisions concerning the proper use
of their land, labor, and capital. Articles typical in regard
to this attitude have been written by M. Ya. Lemeshev, L. N.
Kassirov, G. S. Lisichkin, and V. Venzher.[33] In 1964, Lemeshev wrote, "It is necessary to recognize that no higher agency
can know the concrete conditions and tasks of production as well
as the workers on the farm itself. And since this is so, the
collective and state farms must, in our opinion, be granted the
right to plan not only the sown area, livestock herds, and total
volume of production but also the sale of products to the state."[34]
One writer, L. Ivanov, has noted that in 1964 even though the
February Plenary Session had encouraged local decision making,

still the existence of the state purchase plan and the method of
its formulation in practice limited severely the scope for freedom. "To all intents and purposes, no land remained for other
crops. Under such conditions, the right to independent planning
was in fact nullified."[35] Ivanov does believe that the 1965 decisions to limit the size of the state purchase plan and to keep
it at this given limit until 1971 are overcoming this problem.

Izvestiya, in October 1966, organized a conference to discuss agricultural reforms. A state-farm director, A. Ochirov,
stated that, if given freedom in planning, his farm would imme-
diately alter its production pattern. L. Kassirov, Doctor of
Economics, agreed that this would occur, and he feared it might
have undesirable results in that some goods would not be produced in the amounts desired by the central planners and consumers. "But," Kassirov emphasized, "the economic incentive,
the price, will be in the hands of the state."[36] The desired
total amounts of each good could be called forth simply by altering the government's set of purchase prices. In another
article, Kassirov criticized the 1965 set of purchase prices.
He claimed that the profit level for the average Russian Republic collective farm in recent years amounted to from 3 to 100
per cent and more, depending on the types of output. Certain
products were generally unprofitable. He felt that "a price
policy that takes into account the unequal profitability of different types of output is not only permissible but even advisable.
It should stimulate production in conformity with the planned
rates of growth." However, it was his opinion that in a number
of cases the existing prices did not make it possible to achieve
this. An example he cited is that of milk whose rate of production growth was envisaged by the national economic plan
as higher than that for sunflowers or sugar beets. "At the
same time, the existing prices offer more incentive to produce these crops than to produce milk."[37]

In 1967, about 400 state farms were transferred from their
previous dependence on the government budget to the new
khozraschet, or economic accountability. Within this new
system, the state farms were to bear a significantly greater
responsibility than previously for production decisions. Each
farm would receive bonuses in accordance with its financial
success. The farm's material incentive fund was to receive
15 per cent of the planned profit, but this must not exceed 12
per cent of the wages fund. The social-cultural fund and the
development fund were each to receive 10 per cent of the planned
profits. An insurance fund was to receive 20 per cent of the
planned profit.[38] In 1968 and 1969 this khozraschet system
was extended throughout the state-farm network.

THE PROFIT REFORMS IN PERSPECTIVE

To understand the Russian profit reforms, it is not enough to examine the specific regulations decreed by Soviet political leaders. A number of extremely important questions remain unanswered; and the answers can only be obtained from an examination of actual economic developments within the Russian economy. First, how great will the degree of enterprise independence in plan formation actually be in practice? Will central planners simply add up the intentions of each firm in order to estimate future activities; or will they collaborate in such a way that the rights of the firm will exist on paper only, while the firm repeatedly succumbs to the advice of the planners? Current developments have not yet answered this question, but observers do recognize its importance and many foresee a gradual expansion of each firm's independence. To achieve this, a revision of certain laws may be necessary. This was soon apparent, for example, to Liberman who in April, 1966, wrote,

> It is time to think about how to ensure the rights and interests of the enterprises vis-à-vis their ministries. We must foresee the possibility that a ministry official might try by administrative fiat to intervene in matters in which he has no right to intervene, in matters that the enterprise should decide for itself. . . . There may be a dispute. Though the enterprise may be right and the ministry's representative wrong, the enterprise management will hesitate to enter into a conflict with the ministry to which it is subordinated. [39]

To prevent such encroachment upon the firm's independence, to bolster the strength of a firm's management in a dispute with central planners, Liberman has urged that arbitration machinery be expanded and improved--particularly through creation of a "brain trust" or special staff to concentrate solely on the problems arising in the process of reorganizing the planning and administrative framework.

A second question that still remains unanswered is whether the central planners are capable of adjusting the price structure rapidly enough. Can they adjust prices so as to call forth that amount of each good that is desired at the price charged for each good--or will shortages, with arbitrary rationing, and overproduction, with undesired inventory accumulations, destroy the increased efficiency that is being sought? Can

central planners revise prices accurately enough to foster the
technological progress that the nation's leaders desire? At
several points in this book concrete examples as well as opinions of certain observers have indicated that the bureaucratic
framework for price formation may prove unsatisfactory. [40]
All recognize the importance of this question. In November,
1966, the Chairman of the U.S.S.R. State Planning Committee
acknowledged that "the perfecting of wholesale prices is a decisive prerequisite for a large-scale transfer of branches of
industry to the new work conditions."[41] The Chairman and the
Vice-Chairman of the U.S.S.R. State Price Committee (which
is an organization within the State Planning Committee) have
both described publicly the difficult nature of their task. [42]
They realize that prices must be adjusted continually in accordance with changes in quality. The recent price reform, completed in 1967, required several years of detailed discussions
and calculations. The last overall review of prices, prior to
this reform, was finished in 1955. As the second part of this
book has demonstrated, the success of the new planning framework will be influenced by the rapidity with which central
planners can, in fact, adjust prices and the accuracy with which
they can forecast the results of different sets of prices. The
costs incurred in the process of revising prices may also affect
the desirability of this framework. Soviet experience provides
no assurance that central planners can revise prices rapidly
enough and appropriately enough to elicit the enterprise behavior that Russia's political leaders are expecting.

To what extent will market imperfections frustrate the
efforts of central planners? With monopoly, duopoly, oligopoly, or monopolistic competition, central planners may not
be able to achieve their goals by relying on price setting. Detailed quality standards and inspections may also be necessary.
Legal and financial regulations may have to be altered to permit the entry of additional enterprises into an imperfectly competitive market. To what extent will distortions arise because
firms maximize some criterion other than total profits? What
should be the responsibilities of the banking system, and what
techniques should banks employ to fulfil these responsibilities?

The first part of this book analyzed the shortcomings of the
Stalin-Khrushchev planning system. This discussion indicated
why Russia's leaders should decide to shift their economy into
a new planning framework. Looking only at this first argument,
one could conclude that the detailed central-planning approach
was intolerable and that a fundamental transfer was inevitable.
Margaret Miller, a British economist, has expressed such a

view, claiming that the reforms "will go forward, if only because the retention of present methods involves intolerable
losses to the state. "[43] She believes that the reforms must
result in "an economic structure based on economic rationality
and a real degree of freedom for producers within the broad
limits of the state plan, as well as prices which are not arbitrary but truly reflect the economic costs of producing the commodities to which they are attached. "[44]

The Soviet leadership cannot abandon the Stalin-Khrushchev
planning framework, however, without adopting an alternative
planning framework. Each alternative suffers from its own set
of shortcomings. The problems involved in Western systems
of economic planning, or in the types of market socialism that
resemble them, have been thoroughly analyzed and discussed
in a wide variety of books and articles. The difficulties of decentralized decision making within guidelines set by central
planners have received relatively little examination. In the
1930's, Oskar Lange wrote a widely acclaimed paper in which
he expressed the opinion that central planners could achieve
their goals by setting prices so as to elicit desirable responses
from individual enterprises, each making decisions within the
centrally determined guidelines. [45] The second part of this book
has considered several problems that central planners may
have to overcome if they are to operate successfully within such
a framework. The tasks of central planners are by no means
as easy as Lange predicted. The period of transition to this
alternative system may be particularly difficult, while central
planners become acquainted with their new duties and develop
solutions to the new problems they encounter. The possibility
exists that the Soviet leadership will become discouraged with
their profit reforms and that they will consider the new shortcomings to be even more undesirable than those of the Stalin-
Khrushchev system. Russia may yet move back to its traditional planning framework or onward to market socialism, with
even greater decentralization. Future improvements in methods
of collecting and analyzing information--innovations in computer
technology, for example--may affect Russia's decision concerning which planning framework to employ.

In order to understand and appreciate the recent Soviet
discussions and regulations, it is necessary to realize that
Russia has been involved in a reform movement, and that this
movement is exploring uncharted paths. Russia's leaders have
adopted a variety of original policies on an experimental basis.
It is impossible to predict the economic impact--or the political
and social impact--of many of the new regulations. Hence, it

is likely that some regulations will be discarded, others will
be modified and, in some cases, alternatives will be implemented. Russia may quite possibly take "two steps forward
and one step back," or she may even take one step forward and
two steps back. Basic divergencies of opinion exist in the
U.S.S.R. today concerning the best framework for planning
and administration. It appears that the proponents of the various opinions are willing to settle their differences on the basis
of practical experience as it accumulates in the future, rather
than through resort to political machinations or overt force.
Such a development is important not only in the opportunity it
is providing for free thought and free discussions within the
U.S.S.R., but also in the opportunity it may provide, to other
nations as well as the U.S.S.R., to ascertain more fully the
effects of different methods of governmental intervention in the
economy.

NOTES

1. Sidney Ploss, Conflict and Decision-making in Soviet
Russia (Princeton, New Jersey: Princeton University Press,
1965).

2. V. S. Nemchinov, "Socialist Economic Management
and Production Planning," Kommunist, 5 (March 1964), 74-87.

3. A. N. Kosygin, "On Improving the Management of
Industry, Perfecting Planning and Strengthening Economic
Incentives in Industrial Production," Pravda (September 28,
1965), pp. 1-4.

4. As quoted in Barry Richman, Soviet Management
(Englewood Cliffs, New Jersey: Prentice-Hall Inc., 1965),
p. 230.

5. As quoted in Voprosy Ekonomiki, 3 (March 1963), 78-79.

6. L. Gatovsky, "The Role of Profits in Socialist Economics," Kommunist, 18 (December 1962), 60-72.

7. Ibid.

8. N. S. Khrushchev, "Speech at the Plenary Session of the CPSU Central Committee," Pravda (December 15, 1963), pp. 1-3.

9. M. Kuznetsova, "Demand, Quality, and the Plan," Pravda (October 4, 1964), p. 4.

10. G. Fokin and L. Geller, "Factory to Store to Customer," Pravda (October 8, 1964), p. 2.

11. O. Lacis, "A Survey of Business," Izvestiya (September 23, 1965), p. 3.

12. "Experiment under Examination," Izvestiya (October 21, 1964), p. 1.

13. V. Veselovsky, "Light Industry Will Work in a New Way," Nedelya (October 25-31, 1965), pp. 4-5.

14. O. Lacis, "A Survey of Business," Izvestiya (September 23, 1965), p. 3; as translated in The Current Digest of the Soviet Press, XVII, 38 (1965) 34.

15. Ye. Liberman, "Confidence is an Incentive!" Komsomolskaya Pravda (April 24, 1966), p. 2; as translated in The Current Digest of the Soviet Press, XVIII, 16 (1966) 29.

16. V. Lagutkin, Vice-Chairman of the Russian Republic Economic Council, "Plan Indicators to Stimulate Greater Production Efficiency," Kommunist, 5 (March 1964) 88-96.

17. Ibid.

18. I. Tabeyev, First Secretary of the Tatar Province Party Committee, and A. Grenkov, director of an economics research laboratory, "What Is the Main Index in the Plan?" Izvestiya (February 19, 1964), p. 2.

19. I. Malyshev, Deputy Director of the U.S.S.R. Central Statistical Administration, "What Should Be the Chief Plan Index?" Izvestiya (February 7, 1964), p. 3.

20. V. Nemchinov, "Socialist Economic Management and Production Planning," Kommunist, 5 (March 1964) 74-87.

21. Ibid.

22. See V. Trapeznikov, "For Flexible Economic Management of Enterprises," Pravda (August 17, 1964), pp. 3-4.

23. "The Criterion Is Quality,"--a letter by P. Chervonobrodov, engineer at the Moscow Automobile Plant, Pravda (March 26, 1964), p. 2.

24. O. Volkov, Economist at the Likhachev Automobile Plant, "Urgent Questions," Pravda (August 23, 1964), p. 2.

25. V. Belkin and I. Birman, "The Independence of the Enterprise and Economic Stimuli," Izvestiya (December 4, 1964), p. 5.

26. See, for example, V. Shkatov, a member of the U.S.S.R. State Planning Committee's Bureau of Prices, "What Is Useful to the Country Is Advantageous for Everyone," Pravda (September 1, 1964), p. 2.

27. Ye. Liberman, "Once More on the Plan, Profits, and Bonuses," Pravda (September 20, 1964), p. 3.

28. Resolution of the CPSU Central Committee and the U.S.S.R. Council of Ministers, "On Instances of Gross Violations and Distortions in the Practice of Planning Collective and State Farm Production," Pravda (March 24, 1964), p. 1.
    For descriptions of how "planning from above" has interfered in an irrational manner in daily decisions see, "Concerns of a Collective Farm Village," Kommunist, 2 (January 1964), 58-60; and M. Posmitny, "Thoughts about the Executive's Role," Literaturnaya gazeta (July 2, 1964), pp. 1-2.

29. Ibid.

30. L. I. Brezhnev, "On Urgent Measures for the Further Development of Agriculture in the U.S.S.R." a report at the Plenary Session of the CPSU Central Committee, Pravda (March 27, 1965), pp. 2-4.

31. Ibid.

32. Ibid.

33. For a description and criticism of their views see
S. Kolesnov, M. Sokolov, and I. Suslov, "On the Question of
the Plan and the Market," Selskaya zhizn (September 22,
1966), pp. 2-4.

34. M. Ya. Lemeshev, Candidate of Agricultural Sciences
at the U.S.S.R. State Planning Committee's Economics Research Institute, Ekonomicheskaya gazeta (September 24,
1964), p. 29.

35. Leonid Ivanov, Literaturnaya gazeta (April 6, 1965), p. 1.

36. O. Pavlov, "The State Farms and Khozraschet,"
Izvestiya (October 13, 1966), p. 5.

37. L. Kassirov, "Material Incentives and Production,"
Pravda (January 22, 1965), p. 2.

38. CPSU Central Committee and U.S.S.R. Council of
Ministers, "On the Transfer of State Farms and Other State
Agricultural Enterprises to Full Economic Accountability."
Pravda (April 15, 1968), p. 1.

39. Ye. Liberman, "Confidence Is an Incentive,"
Komsomolskaya Pravda (April 24, 1966), p. 2.
        In this regard, see also A. Kositsyn and V. Laptev
"The Economic Law of the Soviet State," Kommunist, 10
(July 1965), 88-94; and M. Odinets and V. Fomin, "From
Enterprise to [Ministerial] Branches," Pravda (September 29,
1966), p. 1.

40. In addition to the examples and opinions already cited,
see Ye. Liberman, Professor at the Kharkov State University,
and A. Rudkovsky, Director of the Kharkov S. M. Kirov Tur-
bine Plant, "A Plant Working under the New System," Pravda
(April 20, 1966), p. 2.

41. N. Baibakov, Chairman of the U.S.S.R. State Planning
Committee, Pravda (November 4, 1966), pp. 2-3.

42. V. Sitnin, Chairman of the U.S.S.R. State Price Committee, "Price Is an Important Tool of Economic Management,"
Pravda (November 12, 1965), p. 2.
        V. Kuznetsov, Vice-Chairman of the U.S.S.R. State
Price Committee, "Price Is a Stimulus," Izvestiya (November
2, 1965), p. 3.

43. Margaret Miller, Rise of the Russian Consumer (The Institute of Economic Affairs, London, 1965), p. 66.

44. Ibid.

45. Oskar Lange, "On the Economic Theory of Socialism," Review of Economic Studies, IV, 1 and 2 (October, 1936, and February, 1937).

BIBLIOGRAPHY

BIBLIOGRAPHY

Books

Arrow, K. J., and Hurwicz. "Decentralization and Computation in Resource Allocation." Essays in Economics and Econometrics. Chapel Hill: University of North Carolina, 1960, pp. 34-104.

Bolfkabich, S. I., Dubovitsky, L. I., and Simulin, N. A. "The Production of Mineral Fertilizers." The Chemical Industry of the U.S.S.R. Moscow: The State Scientific Technical Publishers of Chemical Literature, 1959.

Chamberlin, E. H. Theory of Monopolistic Competition. Cambridge: Harvard University Press, 1933.

Fellner, W. Competition Among the Few. New York: Alfred A. Knopf, Inc., 1949.

Jasny, Naum. Khruschchev's Crop Policy. Scotland: George Outram and Co. Ltd., 1965.

Mellor, R. E. Geography of the U.S.S.R. New York: Macmillan and Co. Ltd., 1964.

Miller, Margaret. Rise of the Russian Consumer. London: The Institute of Economic Affairs, 1965, p. 66.

Montias, John M. Central Planning in Poland. New Haven: Yale University Press, 1962.

Nove, Alec. Economic Rationality and Soviet Politics. New-York: Frederick A. Praeger, 1964.

_____. The Soviet Economy. New York: Frederick A. Praeger, 1961.

Noyes, Robert. Potash and Potassium Fertilizers. Noyes Development Corporation, 1966.

Pratt, C. J., and Noyes, Robert. Nitrogen Fertilizer Chemical Processes. Noyes Development Corporation, 1965.

Triffin, R. Monopolistic Competition and General Equilibrium Theory. Cambridge: Harvard University Press, 1940.

Wheeler, Geoffrey. The Modern History of Soviet Central Asia. New York: Frederick A. Praeger, 1964.

Periodicals

Abaimov, G. Ekonomicheskaya Gazeta, no. 46 (1963), p. 5.

Alekseveysky, Ye. Ye. "On the Broad Development of land Reclamation" Pravda 28, May 1966, pp. 3-4.

_____. "Land Improvement" Ekonomicheskaya gazeta no. 24 (1966), pp. 36-37.

Alexeyev, M. "Free the Firm from Detailed Controls" Pravda 7, December 1964, p. 2.

Alisov, M. "Urban Potato and Vegetable Shortages: Some Proposals" Kommunist. no. 15 (1963), pp. 88-95.

Aliyeva, E. "Why New Petrochemical Processes Are Applied Slowly." Izvestiya. 8, June 1965, p. 3.

Alpatyev, S. M. Pravda. 1, October 1963, pp. 1-2.

Andreyev, A. "The Harvest Cannot Wait." Izvestiya. 18, July 1963, p. 5.

Arkipov, A. "The Net Income of Kolkhozy and Its Utilization." Voprosy Ekonomici, no. 2 (1965), p. 50.

Anonymous. "Below the Quality of the Best Foreign Models." Pravda, 16 September 1965, p. 1.

_____. "Chemical Land Improvement." Ekonomicheskaya gazeta. no. 24, (1966), pp. 36-37.

_____. "Commission to Summarize Discussion of Economic Questions." Voprosy Ekonomici. no. 3 (1963), pp. 78-79.

_____. "Concerns of a Collective Farm Village." Kommunist. no. 2 (1964), pp. 58-60.

_____. "Direct Contacts." Ekonomicheskaya gazeta. 28, October 1964, p. 4.

_____. "Experiment under Examination." Izvestiya.
21, October 1964, p. 1.

_____. "Improvement of the System of Extending Credit
to Collective Farms," Izvestiya, 26, December 1965, p. 2.

_____. "Next Stage of the Economic Reform." Izvestiya.
22, May 1966, p. 3.

_____. Questions Concerning the Perfection of the Economic
Stimulus for Agricultural Development." Voprosy Ekonomiki.
no. 5 (1965), p. 120.

_____. "Report on the Dismantling of New Machines."
Pravda 7, March 1965, p. 3.

Anonymous. "Strengthening the Rural Economy." Izvestiya.
26, December 1966, p. 2.

_____. "The Economic Reforms." Ekonomicheskaya
gazeta. no. 5 (1966), p. 4.

_____. "The New Economic Regions." Ekonomicheskaya
gazeta. 16, February 1963, pp. 12-13.

Baibakov, N. "Planning the National Economy under the
Reforms," Pravda, 29, October 1965, pp. 2-3.

_____. "The Important Task of Instituting the Economic
Reform," Pravda, 4, November 1966, pp. 2-3.

Barayev, A. Izvestiya, 31, May 1963, p. 3.

Baumol, W. J., and Fabian, R. "Decomposition, Pricing
for Decentralization and External Economies." Management
Science. 11, no. 1, September 1964.

Belkin, V., and Birman, I. "Enterprise Independence and
Economic Stimuli." Izvestiya. 4, December 1964, p. 5.

Belousov, R. "The Emphasis Should Be on Economic Effectiveness," Pravda, 13, November 1964, p. 2.

Berlin, M. "Concerning the Economics of the Construction
of Agricultural Projects." Voprosy Ekonomiki. no. 6
(1965), p. 14.

Berman, H. The Current Digest of the Soviet Press. XVI, no. 23 (1964), p. 14.

Birman, A. "Questions Concerning Improving the Organization of Working Capital," Voprosy Ekonomiki, no. 1, (1963).

_____. "The Economic Reform." Pravda 9, March 1966, pp. 3-4.

_____. "The Reform in Action." Pravda. 21, October 1966, p. 2.

_____. "Thoughts after the Plenary Session." Novy Mir. no. 12 (1965), pp. 194-213.

Bishop, R. L. "Duopoly: Collusion or Warfare?" American Economic Review. L (1960).

Bluecher, V., and Ilyinsky, N. "The Incentive for High Quality." Pravda. 1, June 1965, p. 2.

Borisov, I. "Questions Concerning Specialization in the Manufacture of Chemical Machinery." Planovoye Khozyaistvo. no. 3 (1965), p. 72.

Boronon, A., Lakhno, I., and Totsky, I. "The Repair Industry." Pravda. 23 March 1967, p. 2.

Braginsky, L. "The Bank and Its Customers." Izvestiya. 15, September 1967, p. 3.

Breido, M. "Why the Banker Replaces the Engineer." Izvestiya. 22, July 1964, p. 3.

Brezhnev, L. I. "Land Reclamation Is a Fundamental Problem." Pravda. 28, May 1966, pp. 1-2.

_____. "On Urgent Measures for the Further Development of Agriculture in the U.S.S.R." Pravda. 27, March 1965, pp. 2-4.

_____. Pravda. 2, November 1966, p. 1.

Burenkov, V. Kazakhstanskaya Pravda. 8, October 1963, pp. 1-3.

Bushuyev, V. "The Economy Demands the Development of
    Chemistry." Pravda. 3, August 1965, p. 2.

Bykov, K. "Profit and Profitability." Ekonomicheskaya
    gazeta. no. 1 (1965), p. 31.

Central Committee of the CPSU 1964. "On Instances of
    Gross Violations and Distortions in the Practice of Planning
    Collective and State Farm Production," Pravda, 24, March
    1964, p. 1.

_____. "On the Intensification of Agricultural Production."
    Pravda. 15, February 1964, pp. 1-2.

_____. "Resolution." Pravda. 16, February 1964, pp. 1-2.

Central Committee of the CPSU 1965. "On Improving the
    Management of Industry." Pravda. 1, October 1965, pp. 1-2.

_____. "On the Collective Farm Income Tax." Pravda.
    11, April 1965, p. 2.

_____. "On the Plan for Purchases of Agricultural Prod-
    ucts in the Period 1966-1970." Pravda. 12, April 1965,
    pp. 1-2.

_____. "On Paying for Land Improvements." Pravda.
    20, April 1965, p. 1.

Central Committee of the CPSU 1966. "Directives of the
    Plenary Session." Ekonomicheskaya gazeta. no. 8 (1966),
    pp. 6-7.

_____. "Directives of the Plenary Session." Pravda.
    20, February 1966, pp. 1-6.

_____. "Directives for the Five Year Plan for the Devel-
    opment of the U.S.S.R. National Economy, 1966-1970."
    Pravda. 20, February 1966, p. 106; Pravda. 10, April
    1966, pp. 2-7.

_____. "On the Broad Development of Land Reclamation."
    Pravda. 28, May 1966, p. 1.

_____. "On Raising the Material Incentive of Collective Farmers in the Development of Communal Production." Pravda. 18, May 1966, p. 2.

Central Committee of the CPSU 1967. "On Urgent Measures for Protection of the Soil from Wind and Water Erosion." Pravda. 2, April 1967, pp. 1, 3.

_____. "Concerning the Transition of State Farms and other State Agricultural Enterprises to Full Economic Account- ability." Pravda. 15, April 1967, p. 1.

Charnes, A., Clower, R. W., and Kortanek, K. O. "Effective Control through Coherent Decentralization with Preemptive Goals." Econometrica. 35, no. 2 (April 1967), pp. 294-320.

Chernichenko, Yu. "The Honest Ruble." Pravda. 20, Nov- ember 1966, pp. 2-3.

Chervonobrodov, P. "The Criterion of Quality." Pravda. 26, March 1964, p. 2.

Dergachev, N. "The Economic Interrelationships between Collective and State Farms and Industrial Enterprises Require Further Improvement." Pravda. 4, February 1968, p. 2.

Desiatov, V. "Raising the Quality of Livestock Products in the Sovkhozy." Voprosy Ekonomiki. no. 2 (1965), p. 24.

Domar, Evsey D. "The Soviet Collective Farm as a Producer Cooperative," American Economic Review, September 1966, pp. 734-757.

Doroguntsov, S. "The Enterprise Incentive Fund." Izvestiya. 13, August 1965, p. 3.

Dubovnikov, B. "A Machine Begins with the Design." Pravda. 4, September 1964, p. 2.

Esaulov, P., and Konbratuk, N. "The Economic Efficiency of Agricultural Production." Voprosy Ekonomiki. no. 2 (1965), p. 62.

Etmekdchian, L. "Some Questions Concerning Accelerating the Development of Large-scale Chemistry." Planovoye Khozyaistvo. no. 6 (1965), p. 6.

Fedorenko, N. "An Important Economic Problem." Pravda. 17, January 1965, p. 3.

_____. "Put Chemicalization Plans on a Scientific Basis." Pravda. 16, November 1964, p. 2.

Fokin, G., and Geller, L. "Factory to Store to Customer." Pravda. 8, October 1964, p. 2.

Foreign Agricultural Economic Report No. 13. Soviet Agriculture Today. U. S. Department of Agriculture, December 1963.

Garbuzov, V. "Finances and Economic Stimuli." Ekonomicheskaya gazeta. no. 41 (1965).

Gatovsky, L. "The Role of Profits in a Socialist Economy." Kommunist. no. 8 (1962), pp. 60-72.

Gendelman, M., Slodobin, V., and Azev, S. "Place Economic Analysis at the Basis of Production." Pravda. 25, October 1965, p. 2.

Glikman, L. "Problems in Supplying the Chemical Industry with Machinery and Equipment." Ekonomicheskaya gazeta. no. 45 (1963) p. 11.

Glushkov, V., Dorodnitsyn, A., and Federenko, N. "On Certain Problems of Cybernetics." Izvestiya. 6, September 1964, p. 4.

Gnedenko, B., and Sorin, Ya. "Quality Can Be Controlled." Izvestiya. 21, July 1964, p. 3.

Gnedenko, B., Bashkirtsev, A., and Popov, V. "Reliable Machinery Components." Pravda. 25, February 1965, p. 1.

Gogin, V. "At the Level of the World's Highest Standards." Ekonomicheskaya gazeta. no. 46 (1965), p. 21.

Grossman, Gregory. "About Economic Terminology." The Current Digest of the Soviet Press. XVI, no. 20 (1964), p. 13.

Gunar, I., and Naidin, P. Pravda. 24, February 1965, pp. 2-3.

Gustov, I. "The Bank and Collective Farm." Pravda. 20, June 1966, p. 2.

Gutyrya, V. Pravda Ukrainy. 28 November, 1963, p. 2.

Iakovshuk, N. "Economic Changes." Ekonomicheskaya gazeta. no. 6 (1966), p. 13.

Ismailov, R. "The Yield of Scientific Research." Pravda. 3, July 1963, p. 3.

Ivanov, L. Literaturnaya gazeta. 6, April 1965, p. 1.

Ivanova, P. "What Hinders the Specialization of Kolkhozy?" Voprosy Ekonomiki. no. 1 (1965), p. 155.

Kadyshev. Ekonomicheskaya gazeta. 31, August 1963, p. 17.

Kantorovich, L. "Mathematics and Economics." Pravda. 24, August 1965, p. 2.

_____. Ekonomicheskaya gazeta, 10, November 1962.

Kantselyaristov, P. "Agro-Industrial Complexes in Action." Izvestiya. 14 August 1964, p. 3.

Kapustyan, I. "The Prestige of the Specialist." Pravda. 24, June 1965, p. 2.

Karapetyan, A. "The Tractor." Izvestiya. 12, June 1965, p. 3.

Karmazin, V."Contracts and Enterprises." Pravda. 23, May 1968, p. 2.

Karpenko, I. "What Good Quality Means." Izvestiya. 30, July 1965, p. 3.

Karpov, K. "State Credit and the Development of the Kolkhoz Economy." Voprosy Ekonomiki. no. 9 (1964), p. 51.

_____. "The Bank and the Production Process." Izvestiya. 7, October 1964, p. 3.

Kassirov, L. "A Call for a New Farm Price Policy and Profit System." Pravda. 22, January 1965, p. 2.

_____. "Material Incentives and Production." Pravda. 22, January 1965, p. 2.

_____. "Planning and Calculating Stimuli for Agriculture." Voprosy Ekonomiki. no. 1 (1965), p. 53.

Kazakov, P. "Lagging Production of Fertilizer Containers." Ekonomicheskaya gazeta. 25, July 1964, p. 3.

Kazartsev, V. "The Repair of Farm Machinery." Pravda. 14, April 1966, p. 2.

Khartsiyev, N., and Bazylenko, G. "What Kind of Motor Vehicles Does the National Economy Need?" Pravda. 18, May 1965, p. 2.

Khrushchev, N. S. "Concluding Speech to the Plenary Session." Pravda. 15, December 1963, pp. 1-3.

_____. "Development of the Chemical Industry." Pravda. 10, May 1958, pp. 1-4.

Khrushchev, N. S. "Speech at the Plenary Session of the CPSU Central Committee." Pravda. 15, February 1964, p. 6.

_____. Pravda. 1, October 1963, pp. 1-2.

_____. Pravda. 29, September 1963, pp. 1-2.

Klechkovsky, V. et al. "Rural Areas Await Experienced Agricultural Chemists." Pravda. 12, September 1963, p. 2.

Kolesnev, S., Sokolov, M., and Suslov, I. "On the Question of the Plan and the Market." Selskaya Zhizn. 22, September 1966, pp. 2-4.

Kolobkov, M., Boyko, V., and Laptev, S. "Produce More Fertilizers for West Siberia." Pravda. 9, October 1963, p. 2.

Konovalov, O. "The Basic Direction of the Development of Agricultural Machinery Construction." Voprosy Ekonomiki. no. 5 (1965), p. 3.

Koptelov, V. et al. "Higher Labor Productivity at the Kemerovo Nitrogen Fertilizer Plant." Trud. 28, September 1963, p. 1.

Kositsyn, A., and Lapte, V. "The Economic Law of the Soviet State." Kommunist. no. 10 (1965), pp. 88-94.

Kosov, V. "Send Cheap and Effective Fertilizers to the Fields." Pravda. 9, February 1965, p. 2.

Kostandov, L. "A New Stage in the Development of the Chemical Industry." Ekonomicheskaya gazeta. no. 48 (1965), pp. 11-12.

Kosygin, A. N. "Increasing the Scientific Soundness of Plans." Planovoye Khozyaistvo. no. 1 (1965), pp. 3-10.

_____. "On Improving the Management of Industry." Pravda. 28, September 1965, pp. 1-4.

_____. "Speech to the Supreme Soviet." Pravda. 10, December 1964, p. 1.

_____. "Speech to the Twenty-third Congress of the Central Committee of the CPSU" Ekonomicheskaya gazeta. no. 14 (1966), p. 8.

Koton, M. "Obstacles to the Introduction of the Attainments of Chemical Science into Industry." Ekonomicheskaya gazeta. no. 45 (1963), p. 8.

Koval, V. "The Chemical Industry--Its Importance for Agriculture," Ekonomicheskaya gazeta. no. 46 (1965), pp. 19-20.

Kravshenko, P. "Fertilizers--their Precise Allocation." Ekonomicheskaya gazeta. no. 18 (1966), p. 29.

Krotov, V. Izvestiya. 20, October 1963, p. 2.

Kuramzhin, A. "The Planning and Production of Chemical Machines." Pravda. 18, November 1963, p. 2.

Kuznetsov, A. "Price Is a Stimulus." Izvestiya. 2, November 1965, p. 3.

_____. "The Reform of Wholesale Prices." Izvestiya. 5, November 1966, p. 3.

Kuznetsova, M. "Demand, Quality, and the Plan." Pravda.
4, October 1964, p. 4.

Lacis, O. "A Survey of Business." Izvestiya. 23, September
1965, p. 3.

Lagutkin, V. "Plan Indicators to Stimulate Greater Production
Efficiency." Kommunist. no. 5 (1964), pp. 88-96.

Lange, Oskar, "On the Economic Theory of Socialism,"
Review of Economic Studies, IV, nos. 1 (October 1936) and
2 (February 1937).

Lashkevich, et al. "Give the Fields a New Guarantee of
Fertility." Pravda. 14, February 1968, p. 2.

Lelchuk, V. C. The Creation of the Chemical Industry of the
U.S.S.R. Moscow: Nauka, 1964.

Lemeshev, M. Ya. "Agricultural Planning." Ekonomicheskaya
gazeta. 24 September 1964, p. 29.

Liberman, Ye. "Confidence Is an Incentive!" Komsomolskaya
Pravda. 24, April 1966, p. 2.

_____. "Once More on the Plan, Profits, and Bonuses."
Pravda 20, September 1964, p. 3.

_____. "Planning Production and Standards of Long-term
Operations." Problems of Economics. December, 1962.

_____. "The Plan, Direct Ties, and Profitablilty." Pravda.
21, November 1965, pp. 2-3.

_____. Ekonomicheskaya gazeta. 30, May 1964, p. 13.

_____. Ekonomicheskaya gazeta. 10, November 1962, pp.
10-11.

_____. , and Rudkovsky, A. "A Plant Working under the
New System." Pravda. 20, April 1966, p. 2.

Libkind, A. "Lowering the Capital Costs of Products--An
Important Condition for Intensifying Agriculture." Voprosy
Ekonomiki. no. 11, 1964, p. 28.

Liniachuk, Ya. "Some Questions about Inner-Kolkhoz Exchange." Voprosy Ekonomiki. no. 7 (1965), p. 39.

Lisavenko, M. Pravda. 14, May 1965, p. 2.

Lisichkin, G. "Credit on Faith or Growth on Credit?" Izvestiya. 25, January 1964, p. 3.

_____. "The Limits of a Collective Farm Association." Pravda. 19, September 1966, p. 1.

_____. Voprosy Ekonomiki. no. 7 (1960), pp. 61-68.

Lobanov, P. "Science and Standards of Farming." Izvestiya. 1, April 1965, p. 3.

Loginov et al. "Overproduction of Herbicides." Trud. 23, October 1963, p. 1.

Lomako, P. "The Reform and Technological Progress in the Branches." Pravda. 21, May 1968, pp. 2-3.

Maslinin, S., and Odinzov, V. "The National Significance of the Byelorussian Potassium Basin." Planovoye Khozyaistvo. no. 3 (1965), p. 9.

Malyshev, I. "Planning Is an Important Aspect of Socialist Management." Pravda. 7, February 1963, p. 2.

_____. "What Should Be the Chief Plan Index?" Izvestiya. 7, February 1964, p. 3.

_____. Planovoye Khozyaistvo. no. 1, 1961, p. 48.

_____. Pravda. 20, July 1960.

Mandritsa, V., Bakhtiozin, V., and Smetskoi, A. "Transportation Costs." Izvestiya. 4, July 1965, p. 1.

Martynovskiy, V. "The Importance of Mineral Fertilizers for Agriculture." Ekonomicheskaya gazeta. no. 45 (1963), p. 30.

Matskevich, V. V. "A New Phase in the Development of Socialist Agriculture." Voprosy Istorii CPSU no. 8, (1966), pp. 3-15.

_____. "Aid to Rural Areas," Izvestiya. 28, December 1965, p. 4.

_____. "Economic Problems Involved in the Further Development of the Rural Economy." Voprosy Ekonomiki. no. 6 (1965), p. 3.

_____. Pravda. 15, June 1960.

Mazo, M. "Machines for Chemistry." Pravda. 21, February 1965, p. 2.

Mazurov, K, T. "On Improving the Management of Industry." Pravda. 2, October 1965, pp. 2-3.

Michurin, K., and Fedorov, P. "Trade and Advertising." Pravda. 4, May 1965, p. 2.

Mikoyan, A., and Georgadze, M. "U.S.S.R. Laws Concerning Pensions for Collective Farm Members." Pravda. 16, July 1964, pp. 1-2.

Miller, N. et al. "Gross Output of Roads." Izvestiya. 29, June 1965, p. 3.

Mironov, G. "How the Administration of Industry and Construction Is Organized." Ekonomicheskaya gazeta. 23, November 1964, p. 30.

Moiseyev, M. "Concerns of a Collective Farm Village." Kommunist. no. 2 (1964), pp. 58-60.

Morozob, V. "The Development of Financial Relations in Agriculture." Voprosy Ekonomiki. no. 7 (1965), p. 23.

Moscow City Communist Party Committee. "Pay Special Attention to the Development of Chemistry." Pravda. 4, May 1963, p. 2.

Naidin, P., and Gunar, I. "Put the Application of Fertilizers on a Scientific Basis." Pravda. 24, February 1965, pp. 2-3.

Negovsky, V., and Faizov, K. "Land Is the Farmer's Wealth." Pravda. 14, January 1965, p. 2.

Nekrasov, N. "Distribution of the Productive Forces of the U.S.S.R." Kommunist. no. 3 (1963), pp. 25-36.

Nemchinov, V. S. "Socialist Economic Management and
Production Planning." Kommunist. no. 5 (1964), pp. 74-87.

_____. "Value and Price under Socialism." Voprosy
Ekonomiki. no. 12 (1960).

_____. Pravda, 21, September 1962.

_____. Voprosy Ekonomiki. no. 12 (1960).

Nuriev, Z. "The Grain Economy of Bashkira." Ekonomicheskaya
gazeta. no. 9 (1966), pp. 14-15.

Odinets, M., and Fomin, V. "From Enterprises to Ministerial Branches." Pravda. 29, September 1966, p. 1.

Omelyanenko, De., and Sdobnikov, S. "Give the Virgin Land
Soil-cultivating Machines." Pravda. 16, January 1963,
p. 4.

Orechkin, D. "The Firms Await Scientists." Izvestiya.
20, August 1964, p. 3.

Pannikov, V. "Chemical Land Improvement -- a Dependable
Means of Attaining High Yields." Ekonomicheskaya gazeta.
no. 18 (1966), p. 7.

Parfenov, V. "Accelerating the Utilization of New Capacity."
Pravda. 14, October 1963, p. 2.

_____, and Petrov, V. "The Plan, Profits and Bonuses."
Pravda. 23, June 1965, p. 2.

Pavlov, O. "The State Farms and Khozraschet." Izvestiya.
13, October 1966, p. 5.

Pavlovsky, Yu., and Grigoryev, Ye. Pravda. 24, November
1966, p. 1.

Petrov, N., and Totsky, I. "Spare Parts." Pravda. 25, June
1964, p. 2.

Polyanovsky, V. "Transformation of the Land." Ekonomicheskaya gazeta. no. 28 (1966), p. 22.

Poskonov, A. "The State Bank and the Economy." Izvestiya.
25, March 1965, p. 5.

Posmitny, M. "Thoughts about the Executive's Role." Literaturnaya gazeta, 2, July 1964, pp. 1-2.

Prudnikova, B. Sovetskaya Moldaviya. 12, October 1963,
p. 3; translated in OTS; 64-21121, U.S.S.R. Industrial
Development, no. 130, pp. 8-10.

Radov, G. "In and around the Villages." Literaturnaya gazeta.
18, October 1966, pp. 2-3; 20, October 1966, pp. 1-2.

"Report on the Rustavi Nitrogen Fertilizer Plant." in J.P.R.S.;
22,780; O.T.S.: 64-21317; The Soviet Chemical Industry.
no. 138 17, January 1964.

Richman, Barry M. Soviet Management. Englewood Cliffs,
New Jersey: Prentice-Hall, Inc., 1965.

Romanov, G. "Collaboration between Science and Industry."
Izvestiya. 28, March 1965, p. 2.

Roshkov, V. "The Troubles of the Soligorsk Chemists."
Ekonomicheskaya gazeta. no. 26 (1966), p. 8.

Rothschild, K. W. "Price Theory and Oligopoly." Economic
Journal. LVII (1947).

Sadovsky, Ye. Sovetskaya Byelorussia. October 18, 1963,
p. 2; translated in J.P.R.S.; 22,671; O.J.S.; 64-21248;
U.S.S.R. Industrial Development. no. 133, 9, January
1964, p. 15.

Savinykh, A. "Putting Electricity into Fields and Livestock
Quarters," Pravda, 17, September 1965, p. 2.

Sdobnikov, S., and Onelyanenko, De. "Give the Virgin Land
New Machines for Cultivation." Pravda. 16, January 1963,
p. 4.

Sel'skoe Khozyaistvo SSSR. Moscow, 1960.

Serebrennikov, P., "Problems of Procurement and Processing
of Livestock Products." Problems of Economics. February
1959, p. 42.

Sergeyev, Yu., and Tereshchenko, Q. "New Technology and Patents." Kommunist. no. 8 (1965), pp. 65-72.

Shestakov, A. "The Quality of Vitamins of the Fields." Ekonomicheskaya gazeta. no. 19 (1965), p. 14.

Shkatov, V. "What Is Useful for the Country Is Advantageous for Everyone." Pravda. 1, September 1964, p. 2.

Shubik, M. "Incentives, Decentralized Control, The Assignment of Joint Costs and Internal Pricing." Cowles Foundation Paper, no. 178, New Haven: Yale University, 1962.

Shubladze, K. K. "Mineral Fertilizers and Irrigation Guarantee Large Harvests." Pravda. 29, September 1963, pp. 1-2.

Sitnin, V. "Price Is an Important Tool of Economic Management. Pravda. 12, November 1965, p. 2.

Skalov, K., and Molyarchuk, T. "How Should the Delivery of Mineral Fertilizers Be Organized?" Ekonomicheskaya gazeta. no. 35 (1965), p. 15.

Skrebtsov, A. "The Plant and the New Machine." Pravda. 15, September 1965, p. 4.

Smirnitsky, E. "The Organization of Research and the Application of Its Results." Ekonomicheskaya gazeta. no. 50 (1965), p. 9.

Snieckus, A. "Towards a Close Alliance between Science and Production." Pravda. 18, April 1965, p. 2.

Sofronov, V. "Design Errors at the Sredneural'sk Copper Smelting Plant." Ekonomicheskaya gazeta. no. 33 (1963), p. 11.

Stigler, G. J. "The Kinky Oligopoly Demand Curve and Rigid Prices." Journal of Political Economy, LV (1947).

Sweezy, P. M. "Demand under Conditions of Oligopoly." Journal of Political Economy, XLVII, 1939.

Tabeyev, F. "The Agro-Industrial Complex." Izvestiya. 4, March 1964, p. 3.

_____, and Grenkov, A. "What Should Be the Main Index in the Plan ?" Izvestiya. 19, February 1964, p. 2.

Taponenko, T. "Democratic Centralization in Planning the Agricultural Economy." Planovoye Khozyaistvo. no. 1 (1965), p. 18.

_____. "The Economic Condition Necessary for Developing Agriculture." Planovoye Khozyaistvo. no. 5 (1965), p. 7.

"The Maardu Chemical Combine." J.P.R.S.: 22,805; O.J.S.: 64-21337; The Soviet Chemical Industry. no. 139, 20, January 1964.

Tonurist, E. "Collective Farm Wage Payments." Izvestiya. 8, May 1964, p. 3.

Tramoteva, L., and Kalashnikova, I. "The Development of the Oil-Chemical Complex of Transcaucasia." Planovoye Khozyaistvo. no. 11 (1965), p. 44.

Trapeznikov, V. "For Flexible Economic Management of Enterprises." Pravda. 17, August 1964, pp. 3-4.

_____. "The Quality Criterion." Pravda. 20, October 1963, p. 4.

Tselinny Krai editors, Pravda. 5, August 1965, p. 2.

Ushakov, V. "Credit, Economy, and Profit." Izvestiya. 7, October 1964, p. 3.

U.S.S.R. Council of Ministers. Pravda. 11, April 1965, p. 1.

Valayev, N. "What Is Retarding the Development of Chemical Machine Building?" 23, September 1964, p. 2.

Valushenich, E. "Attempts at Raising the Profitability of Livestock." Planovoye Khozyaistvo. no. 7 (1965), p. 53.

Vasilenko, M., and Kolesnev, S. "Problems of Utilization of Labor in the Countryside." Kommunist. no. 18 (1965), pp. 65-74.

Veselovsky, V. "Light Industry Will Work in a New Way."
Nedelya. 25-31, October 1964, pp. 4-5.

Voinov, K. "Status of Construction at the Volzhsky Chemical
Combine." Trud, 29, November 1963, p. 1.

Volkov, O. "Urgent Questions." Pravda. 23, August, 1964,
p. 2.

Volovchenko, I. Izvestiya. 19, January 1966, p. 5.

Voluisky, N. "The Turnover Tax and Financial Stimuli of
Production." Ekonomicheskaya gazeta. no. 40 (1964), p. 11.

Voronin, A. "Combining Agriculture and Industrial Production
in the Countryside." Problems of Economics. January 1962,
p. 34.

Vukovich, V. "The Experiment in Its Initial Phase." Izvestiya.
26, December 1965, p. 3.

Ward, Benjamin. "The Firm in Illyria; Market Syndicalism."
American Economic Review. September 1958, pp. 566-589.

Yarmoshchuk, G., Gunemchuk, P., and Prishlyak, V.
Izvestiya. 7, September 1963, p. 3.

Yefimov, A. "A Method for Improving Plans." Izvestiya.
7, September 1963, p. 3.

Yegorushkin, V., and Sharov, V. "The Tractor on the Collective Farm." Pravda. 15, May 1965, p. 2.

Yermolenko, N., and Pavlyuchenko, M. "Byelorrussia Needs
Mineral Fertilizers." Izvestiya. 21, May 1958, p. 3.

Zaitsev, R. Komsomolskaya Pravda. 13, October 1966, p. 2.

Zaudalov, A., and Blokh, V. "Plans and Possibilities of
Virgin Land Farming." Pravda. 15, June 1965, p. 2.

Zotov, M. "Credit under the New Reform." Izvestiya.
20, October 1966, p. 3.

ABOUT THE AUTHOR

David W. Conklin is an assistant professor in the Depart-
ment of Economics, University of Western Ontario in London,
Canada. He has done research and consulting work for the
Canadian Royal Commission on Farm Machinery, the Treasury
Department of the Ontario Government, the Canadian Inter-
national Development Agency, and private corporations.
His articles have appeared in Soviet Studies and The Canadian
Journal of Economics.

Dr. Conklin received his undergraduate education at the
University of Toronto and was awarded the Ph. D. by the
Massachusetts Institute of Technology.